Angel Lust

Volume 2

Illustration by
Anibal Maraschi

A GALLERY GIRLS COLLECTION

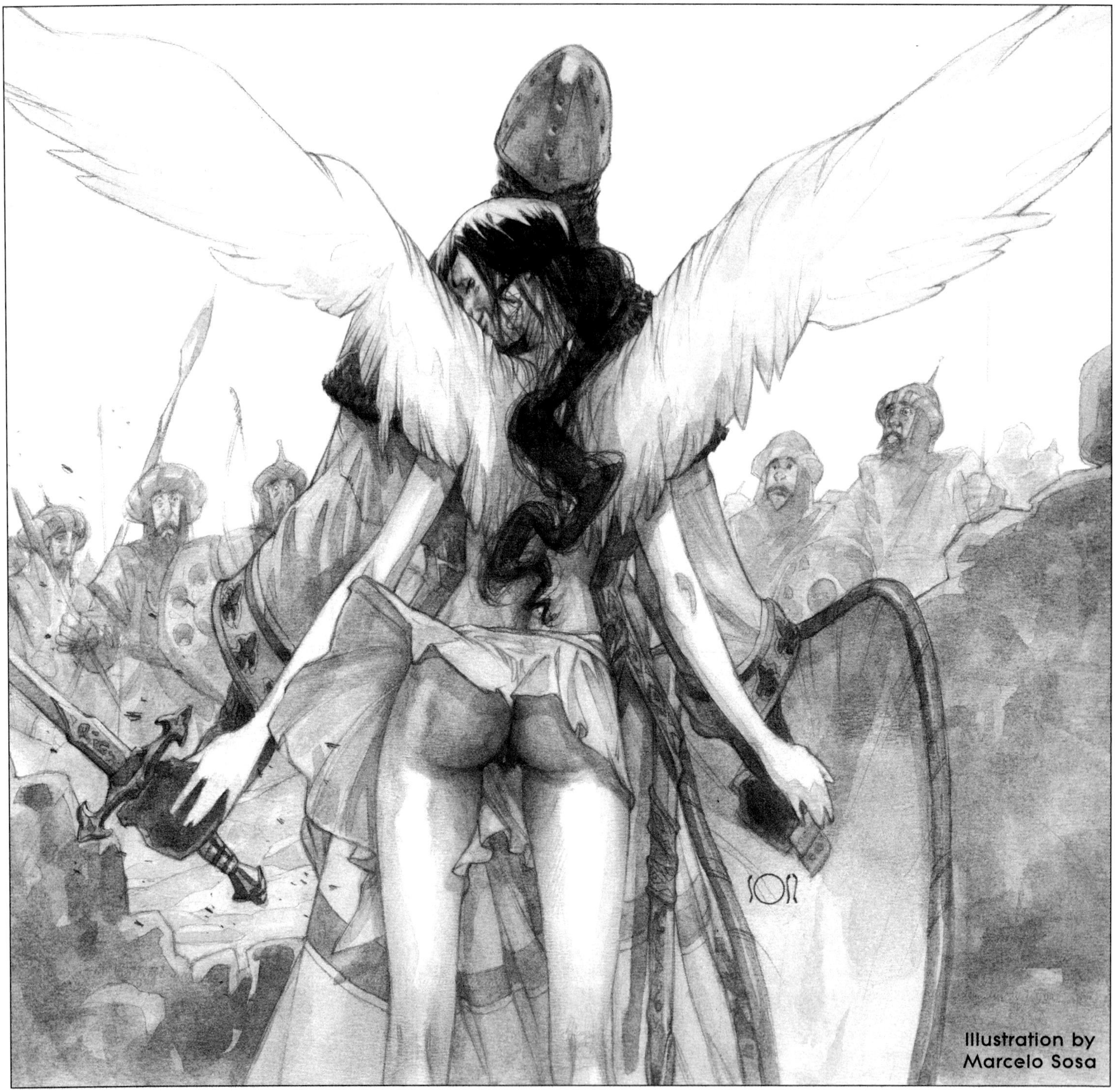

Illustration by
Marcelo Sosa

ANGEL LUST

Volume Two

Book design by Grassy Knoll Studios.

Published by
SQP Inc.
PO Box 248 - Columbus, NJ 08022

Sal Quartuccio & Bob Keenan - Publishers

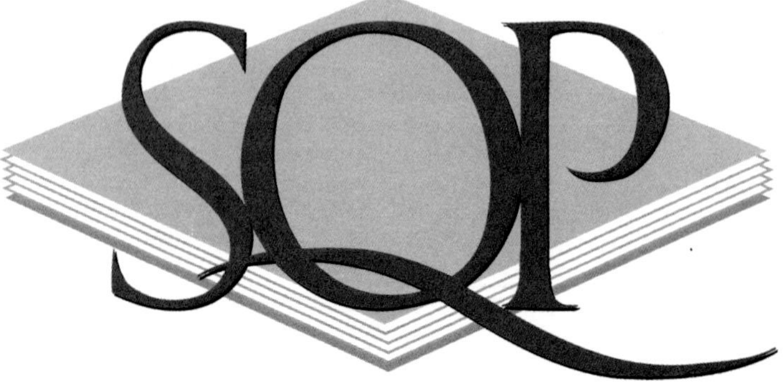

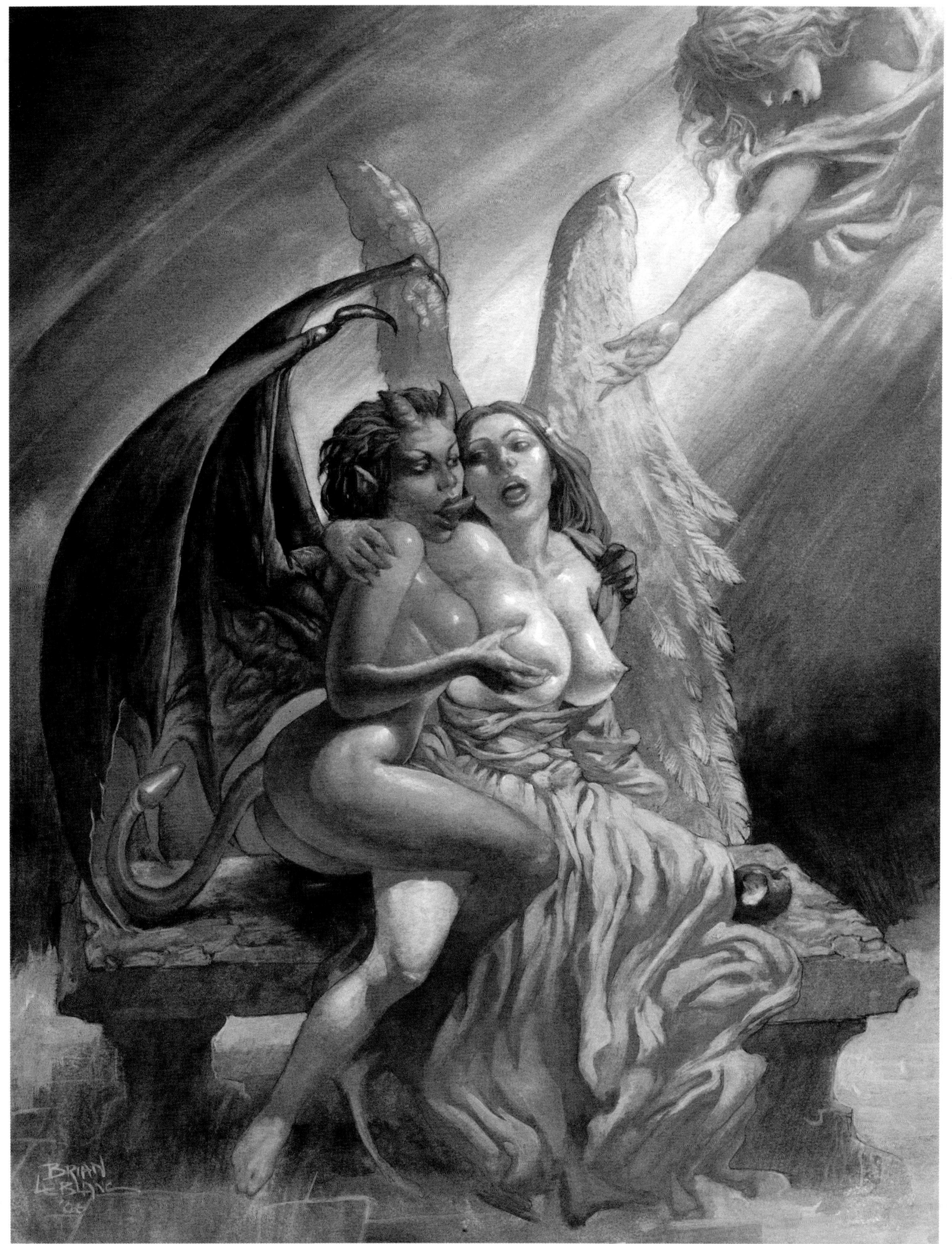

Brian LeBlanc

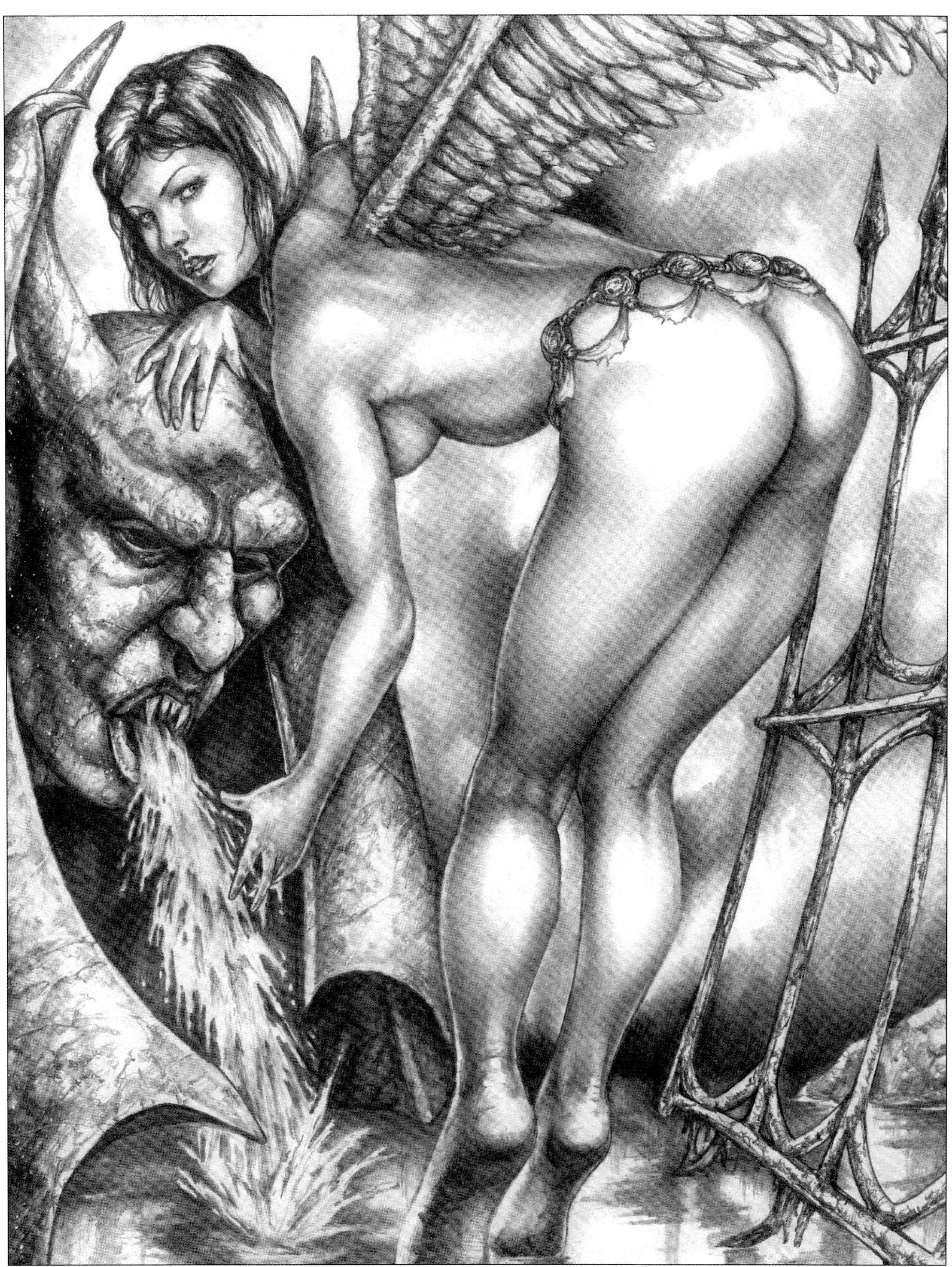

Diego Cândia

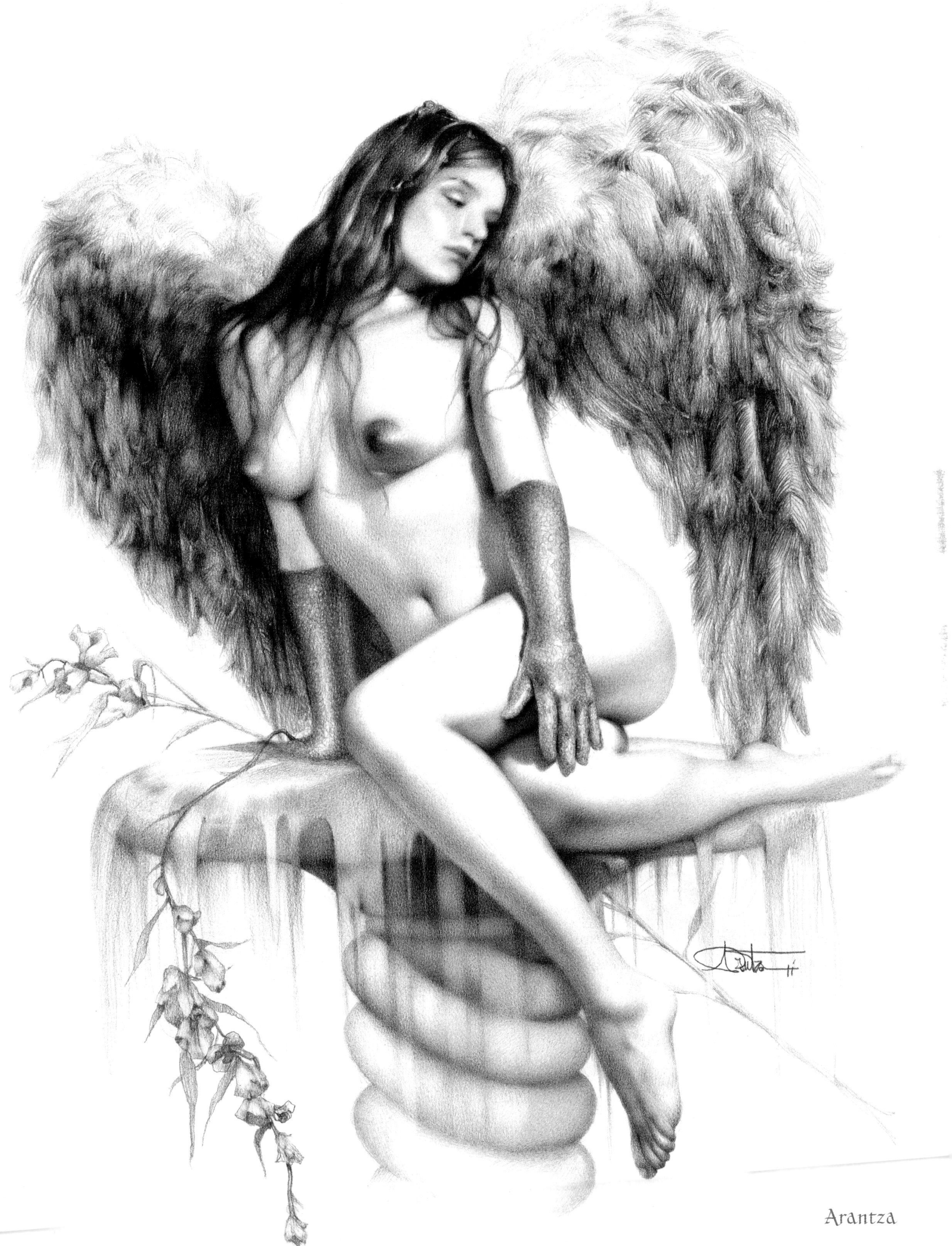

Arantza

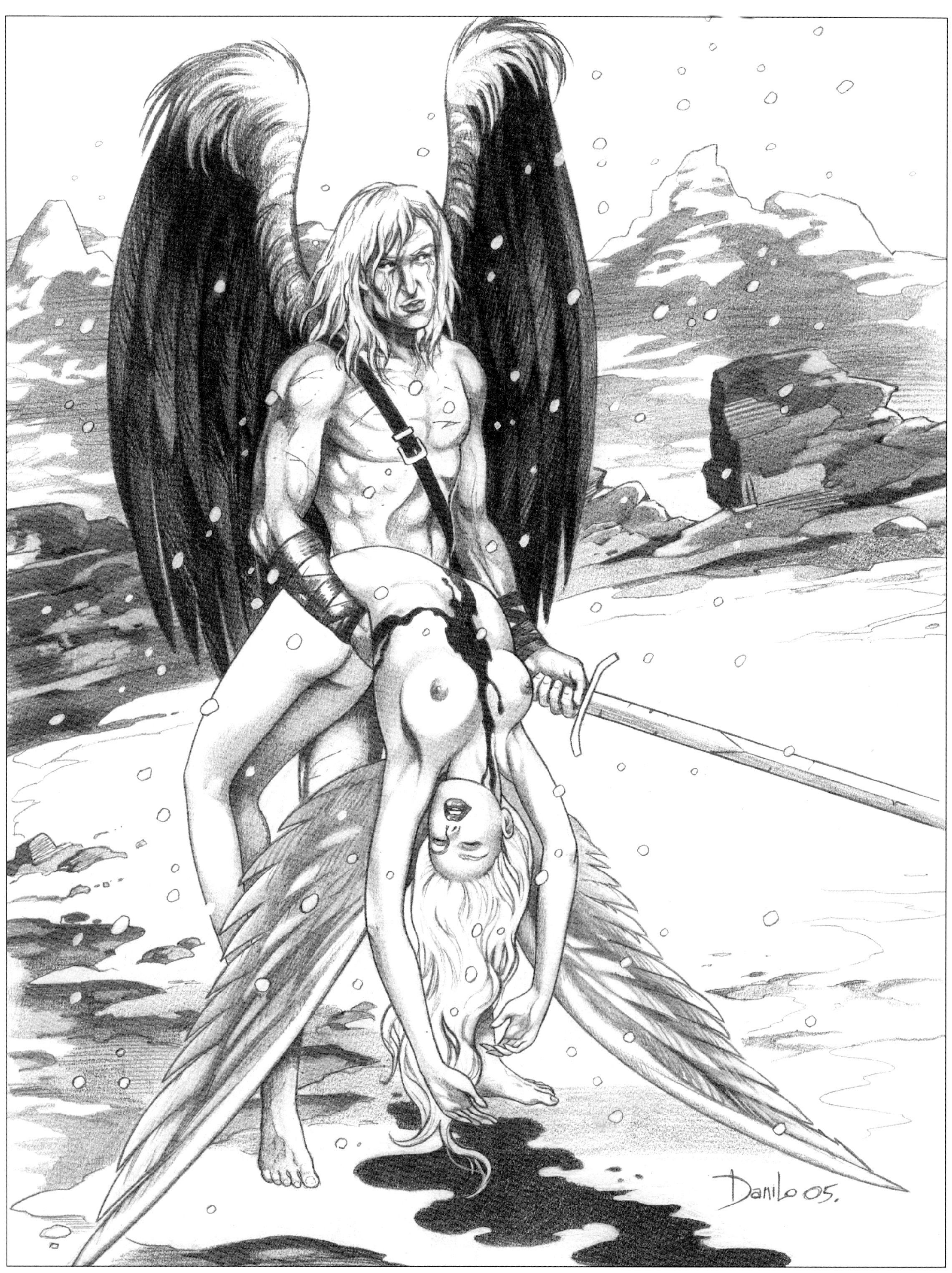

Danilo Guida

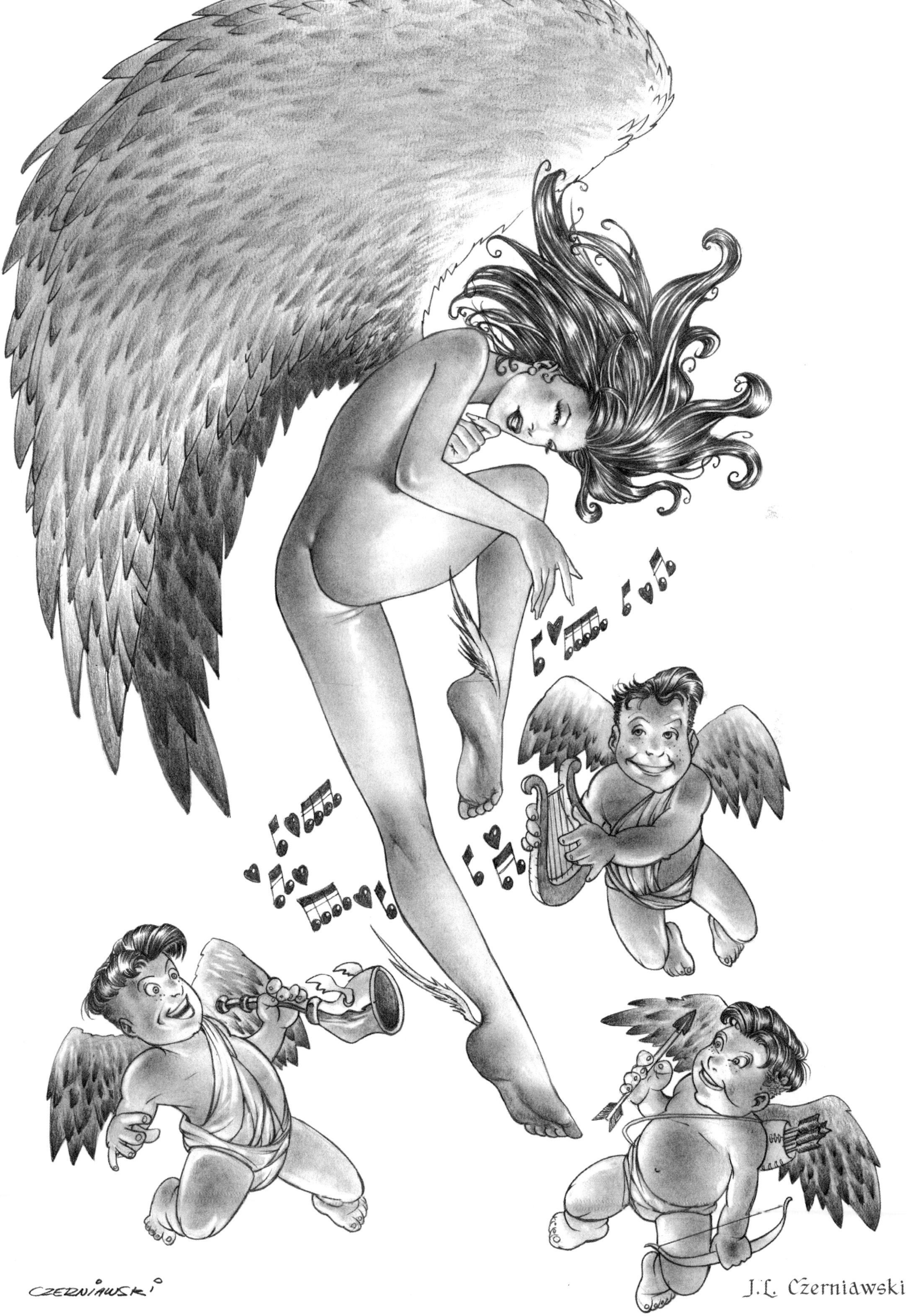

CZERNIAWSKI

J.L. Czerniawski

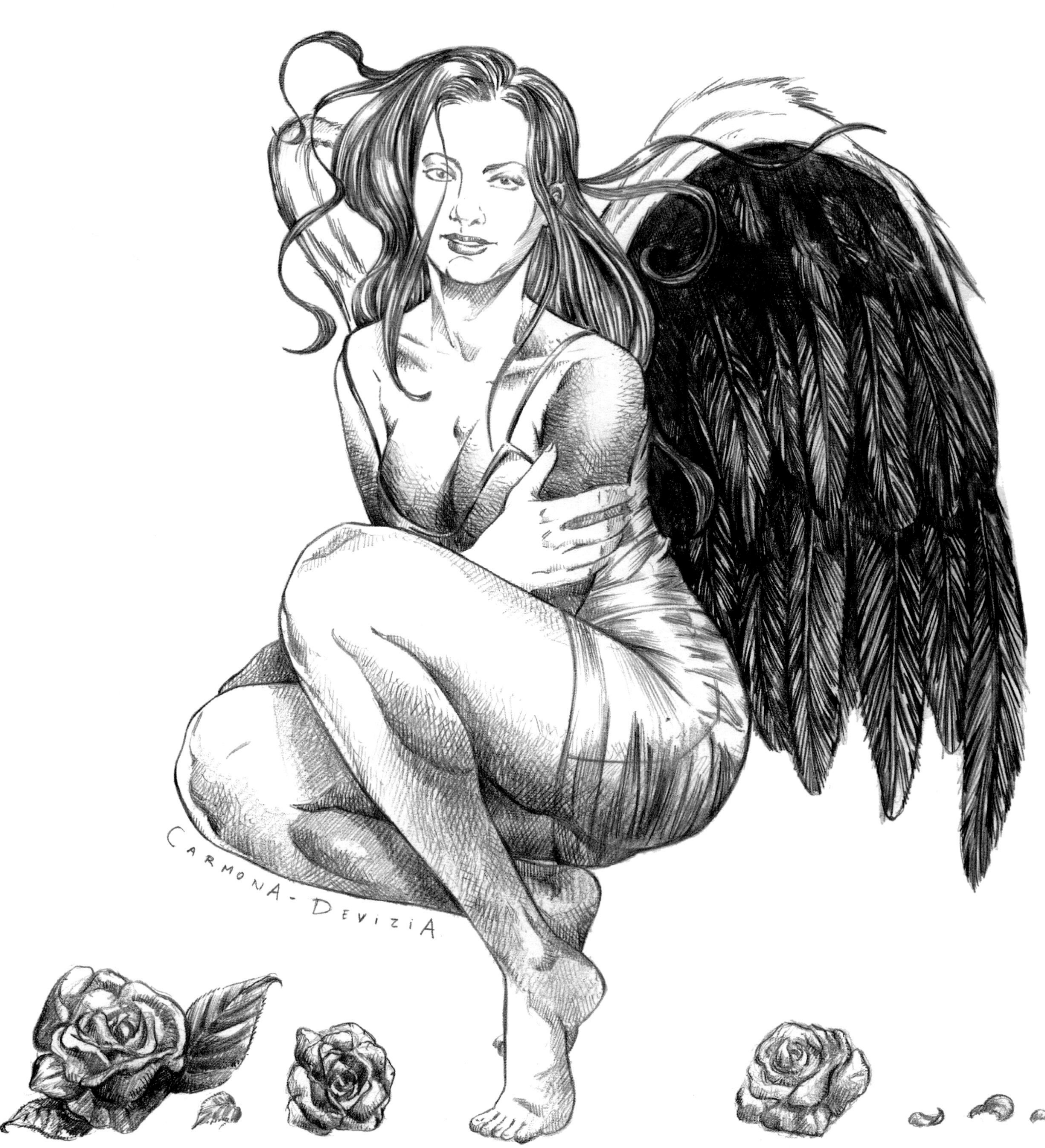

Carmona/Devizia

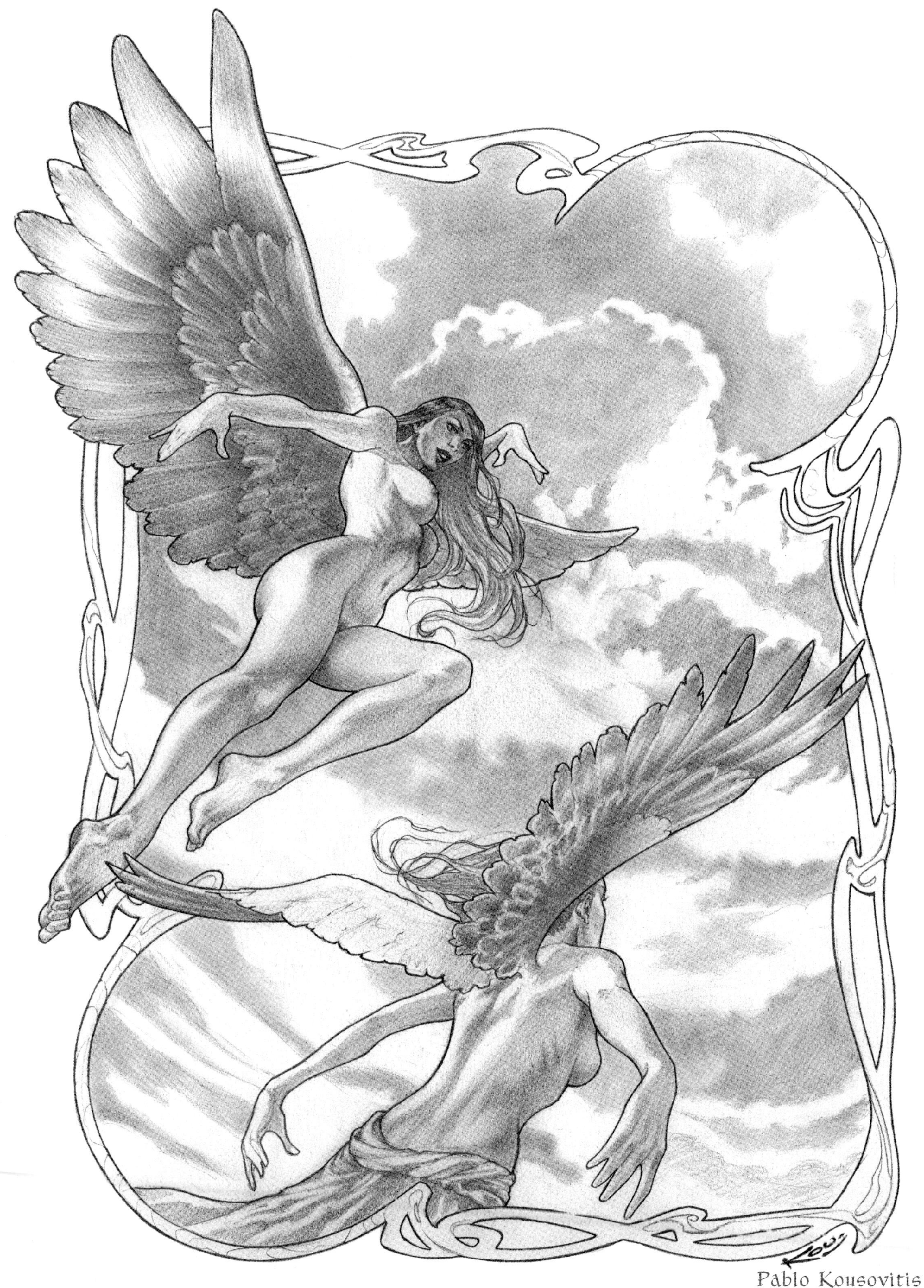

Pablo Kousovitis

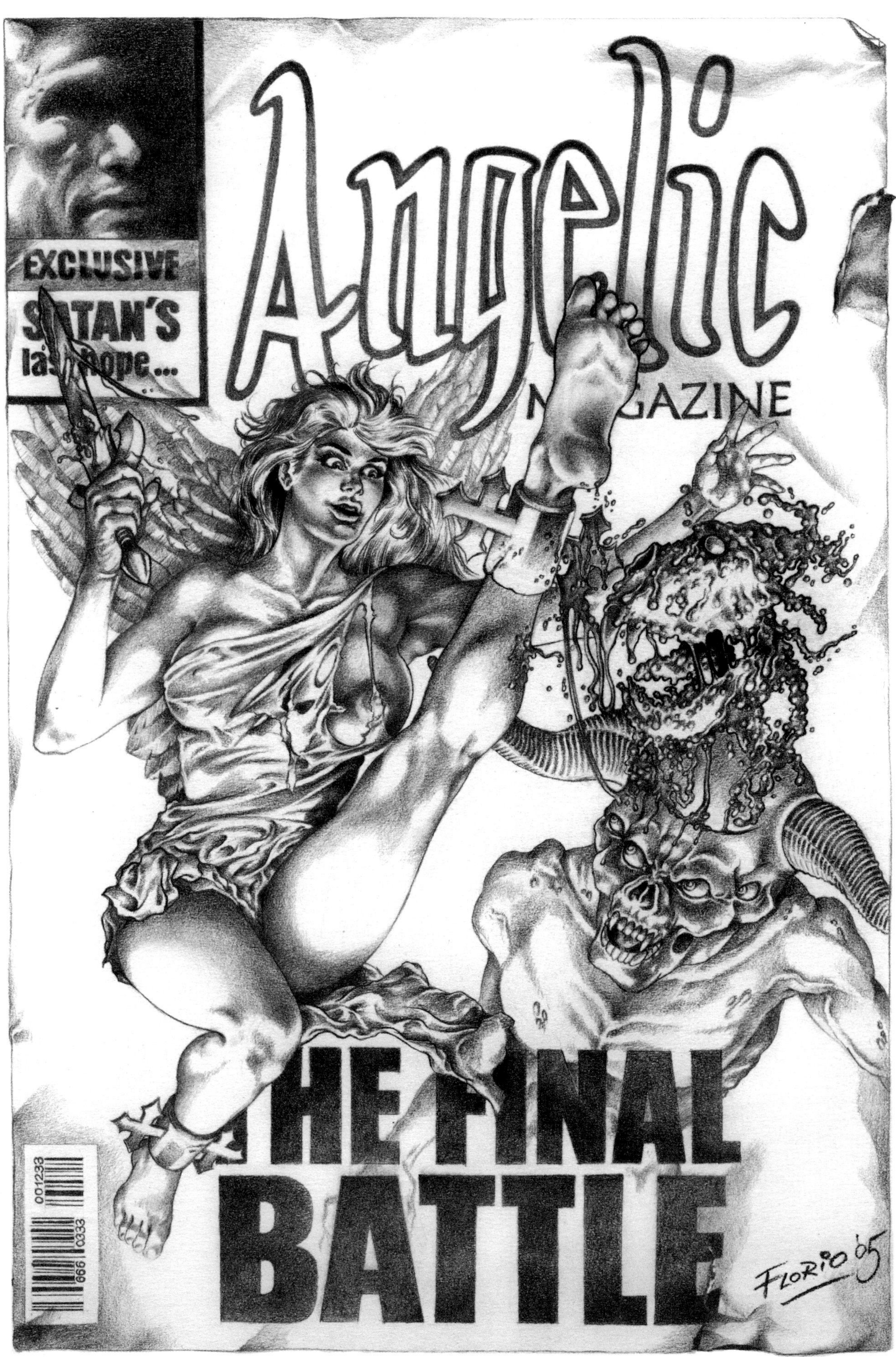

Diego Florio

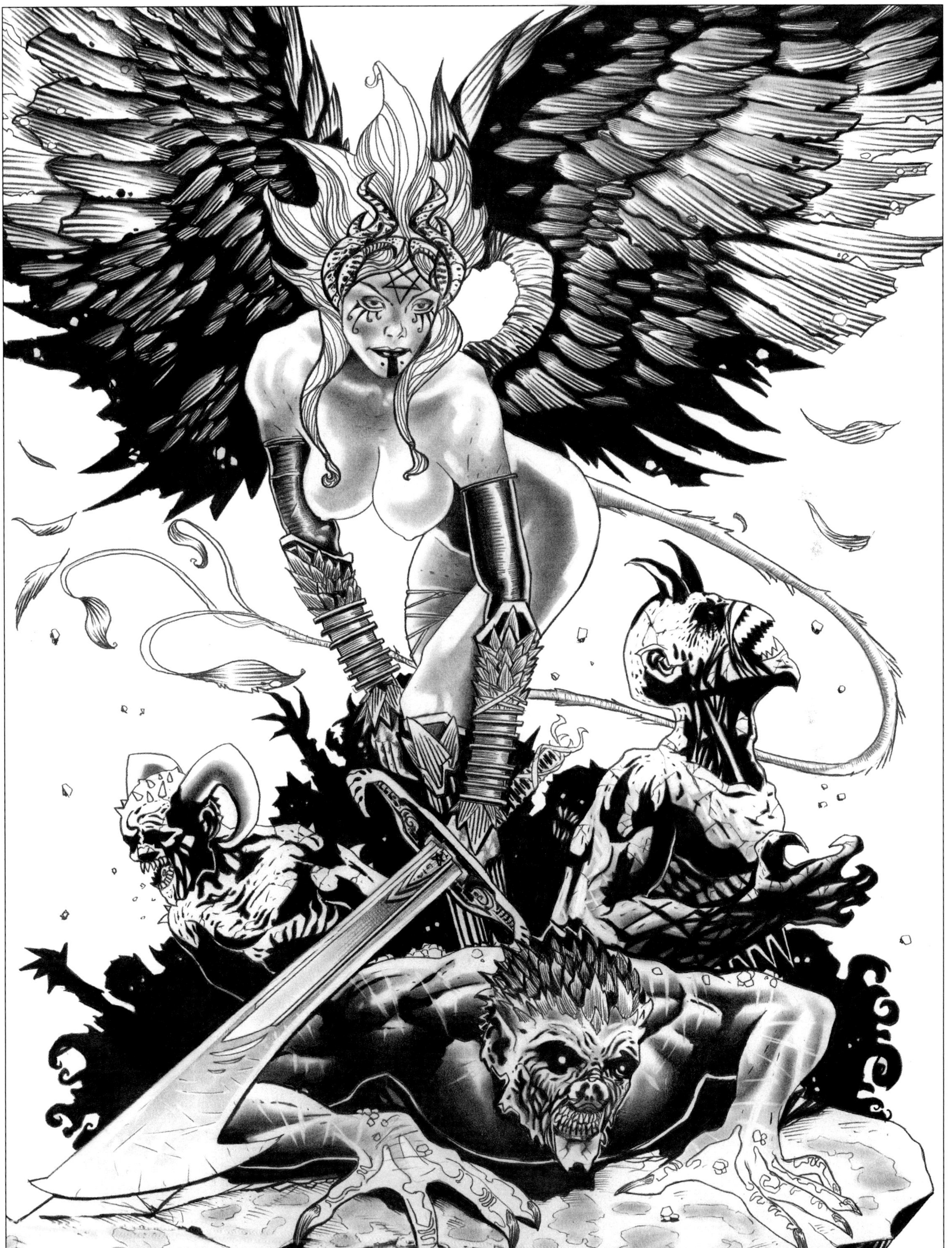

Luis Buci

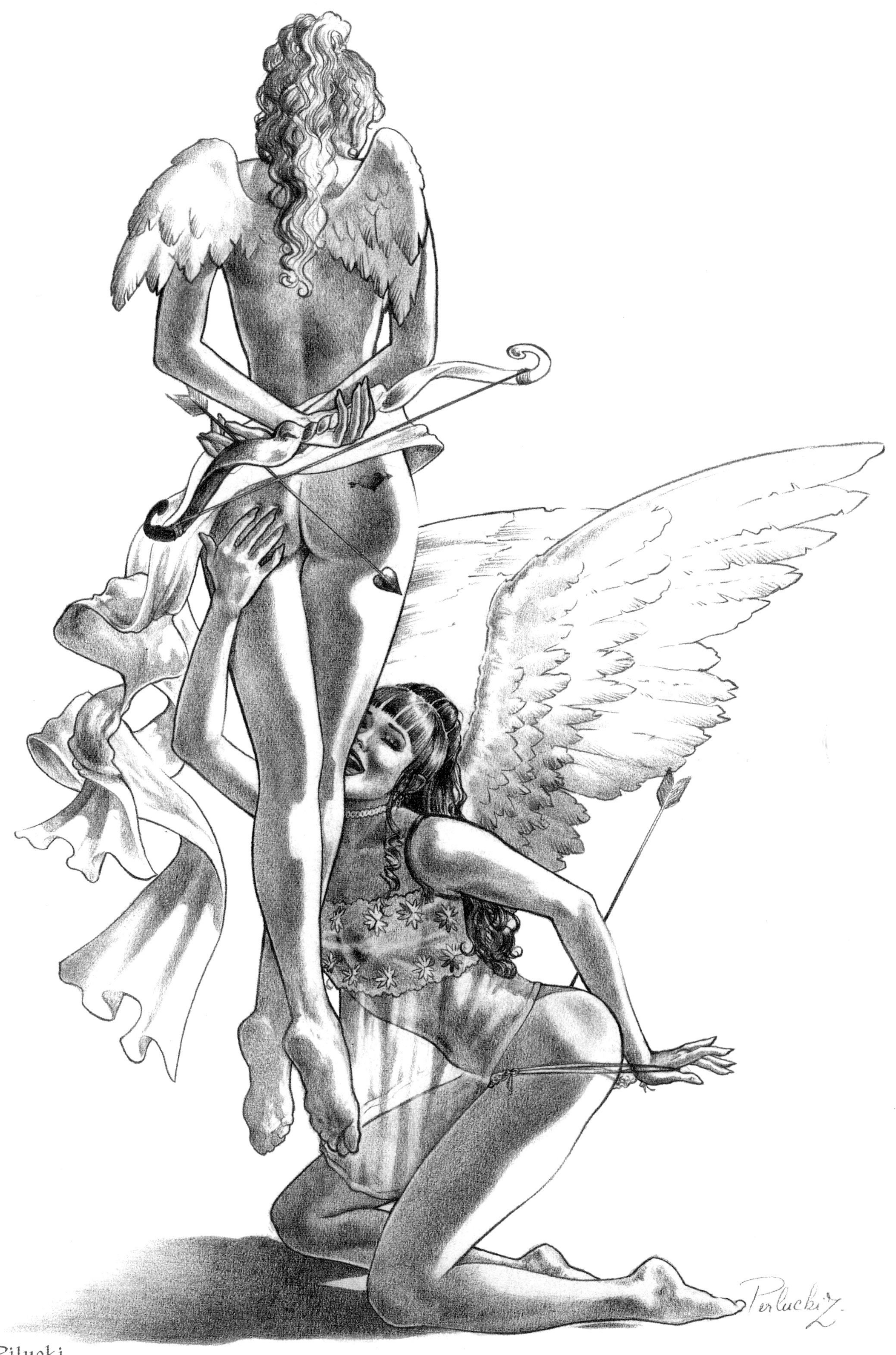

Perla Pilucki

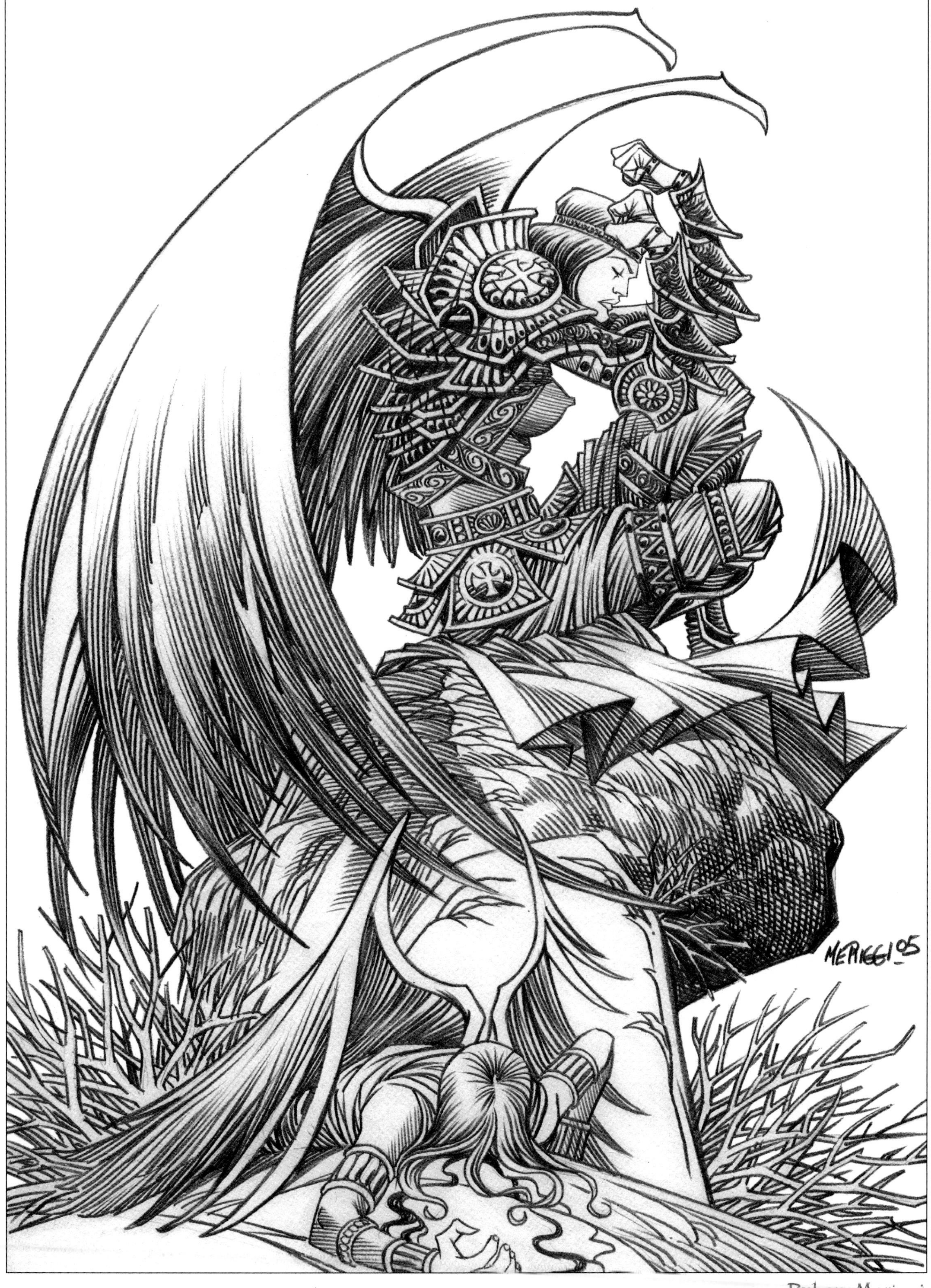

Ruben Meriggi

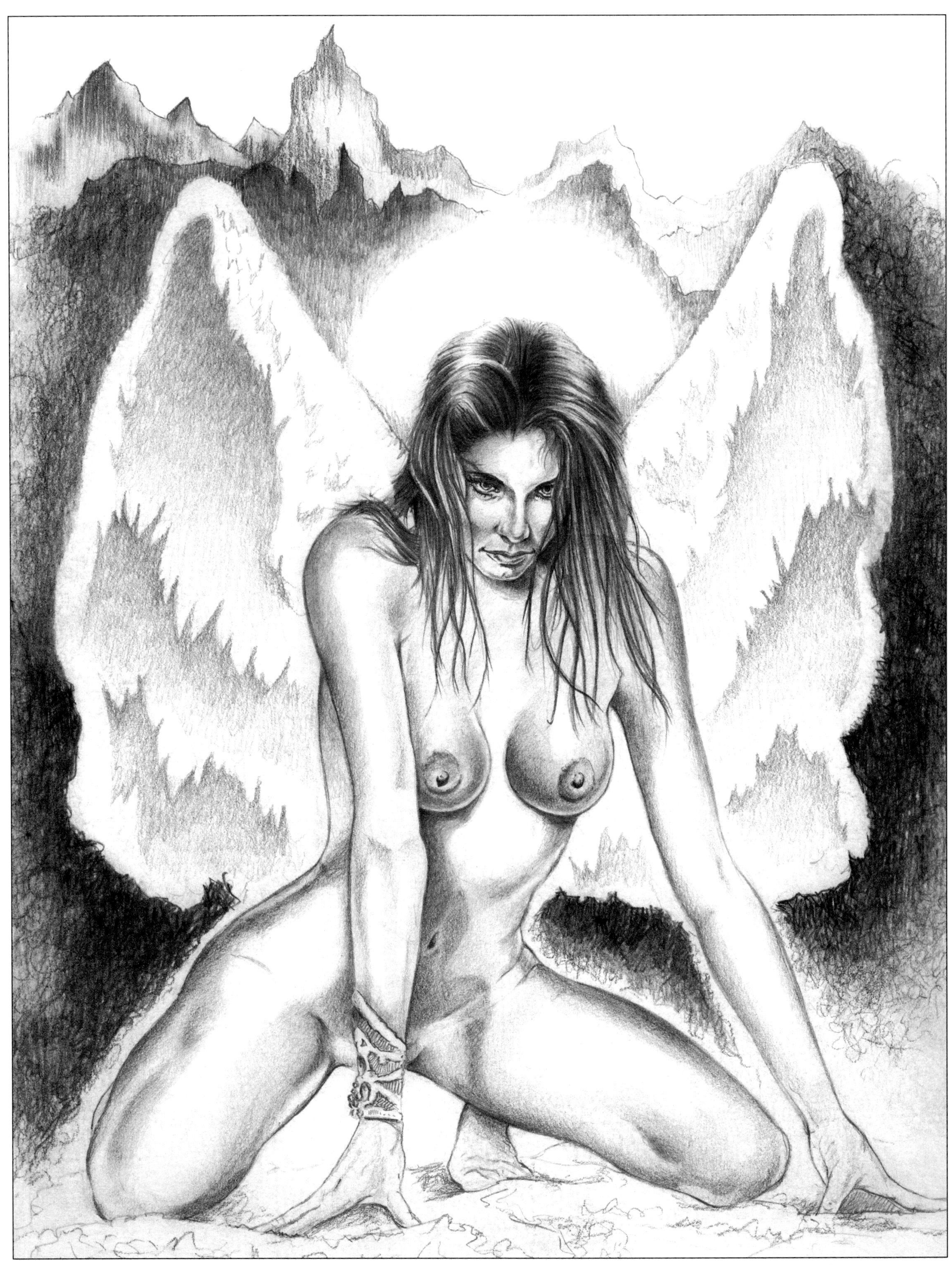

Oscar Gârcia

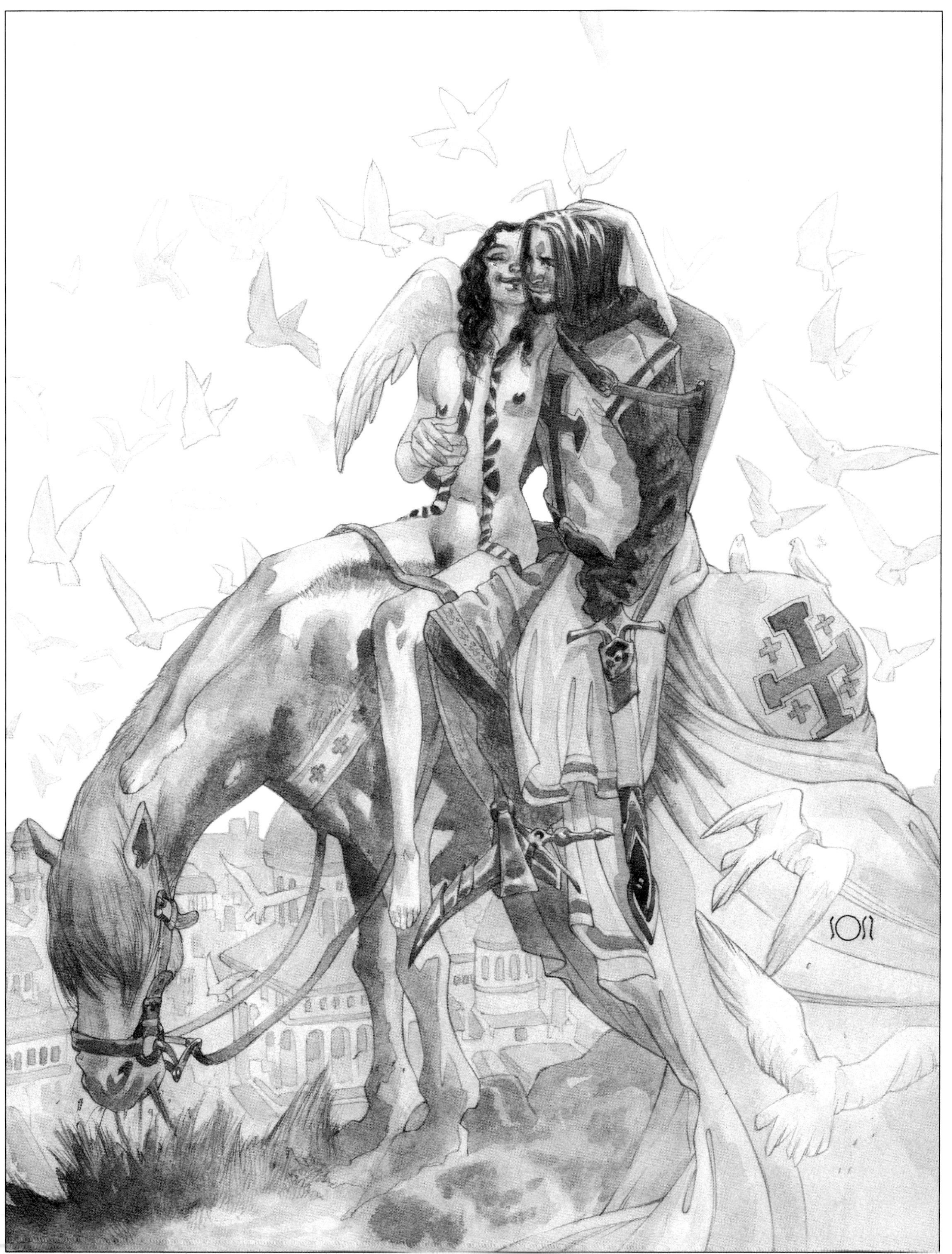

Marcelo Sosa

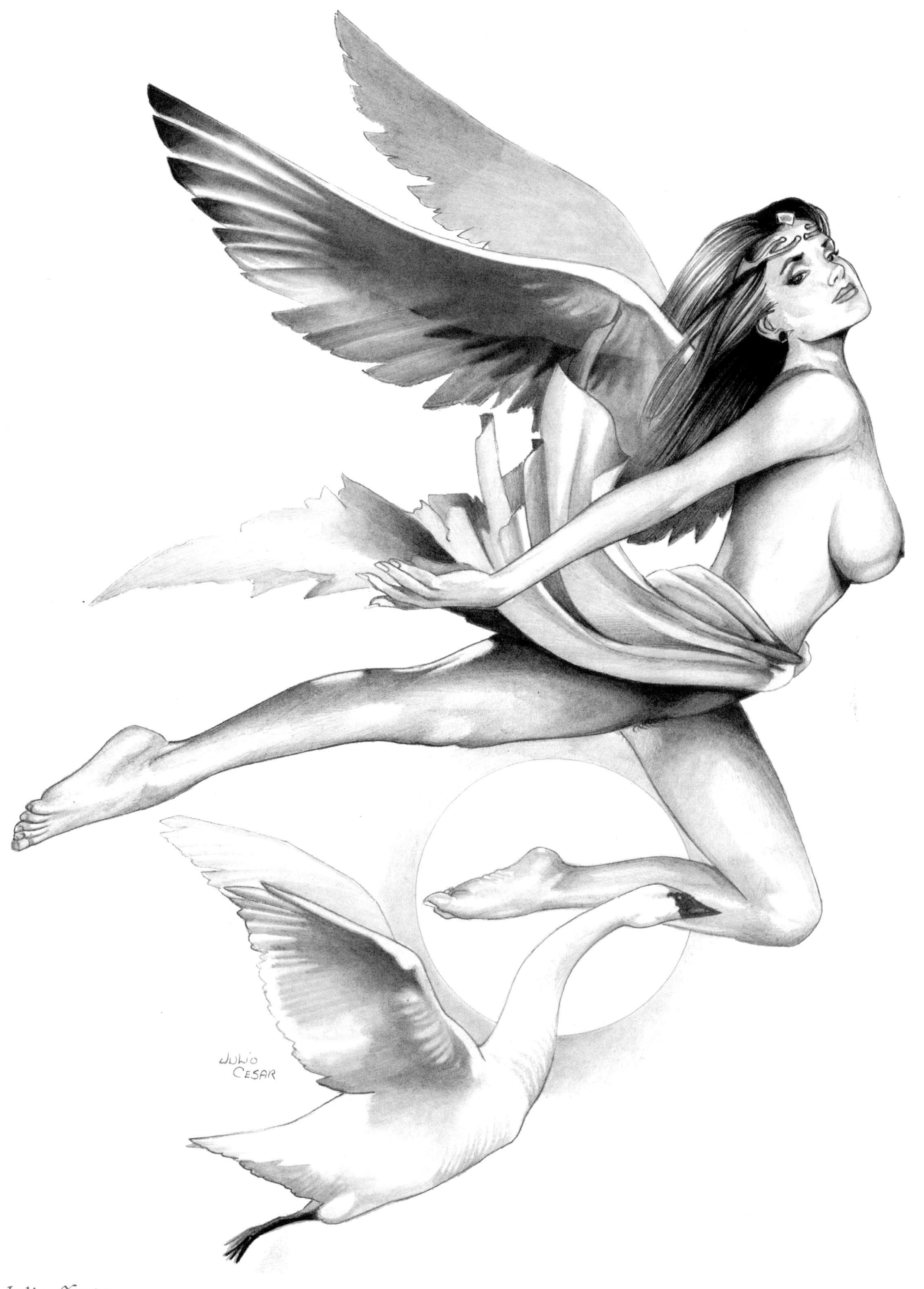

Julio Cesar

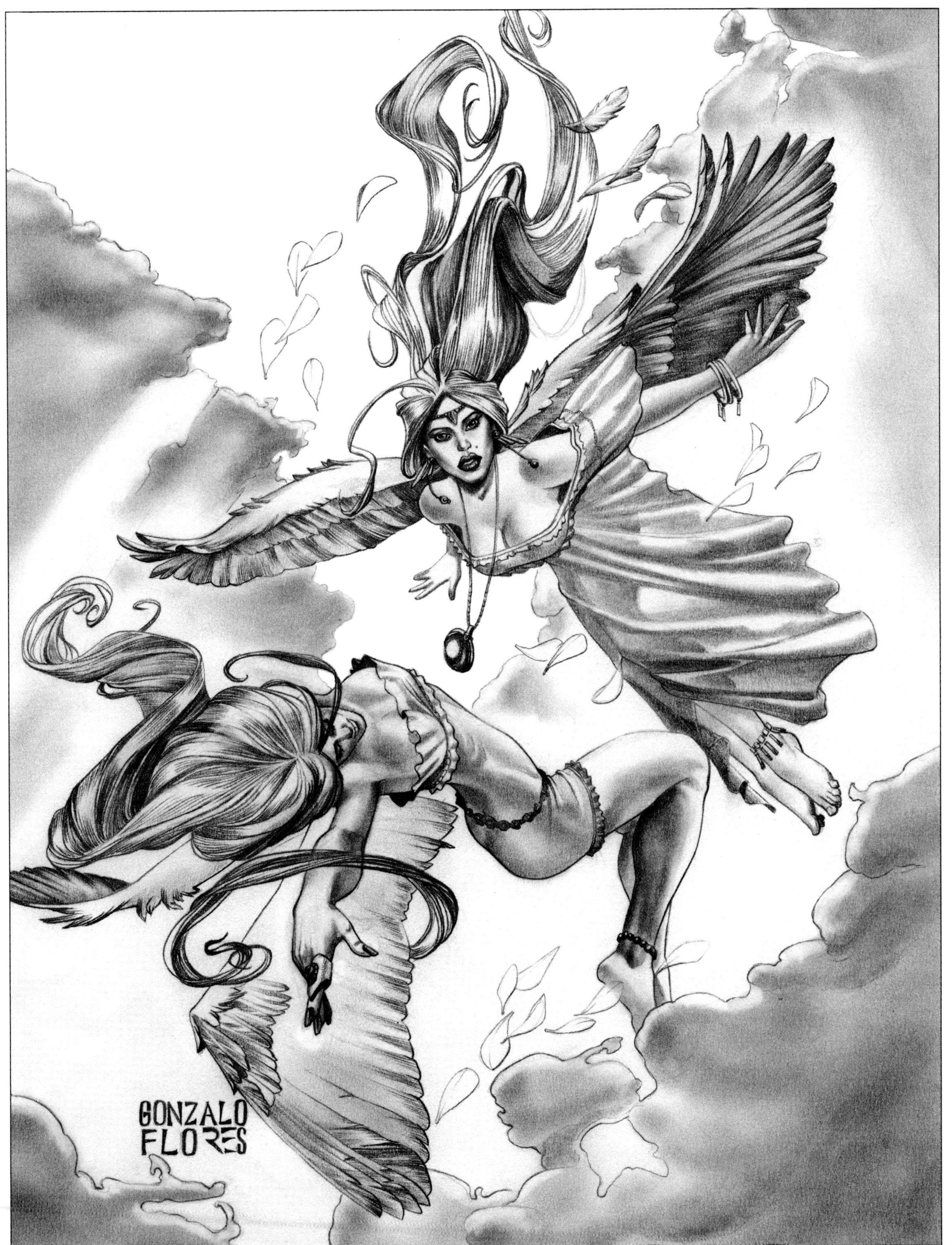

Gonzalo Flores

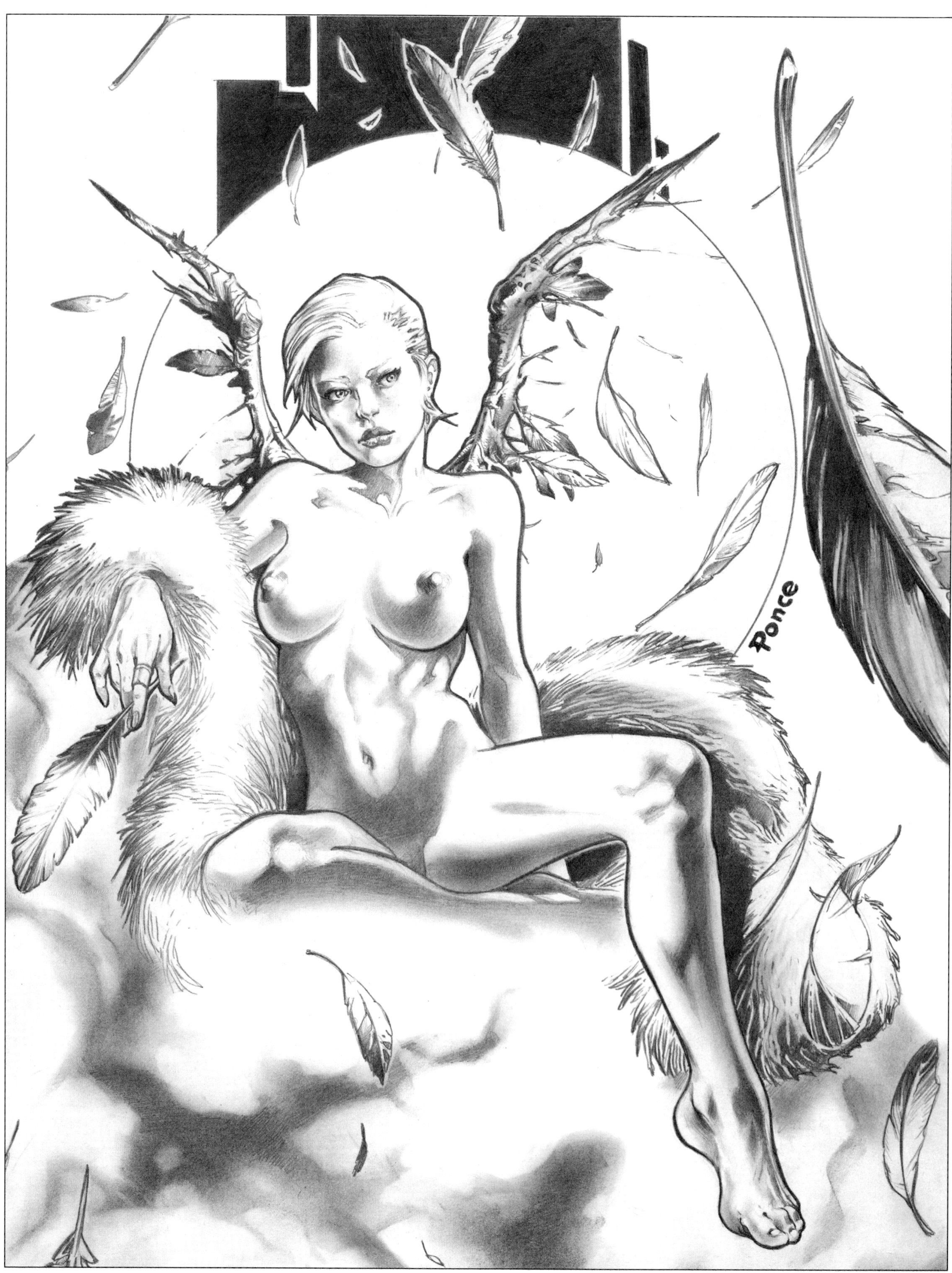

German Ponce

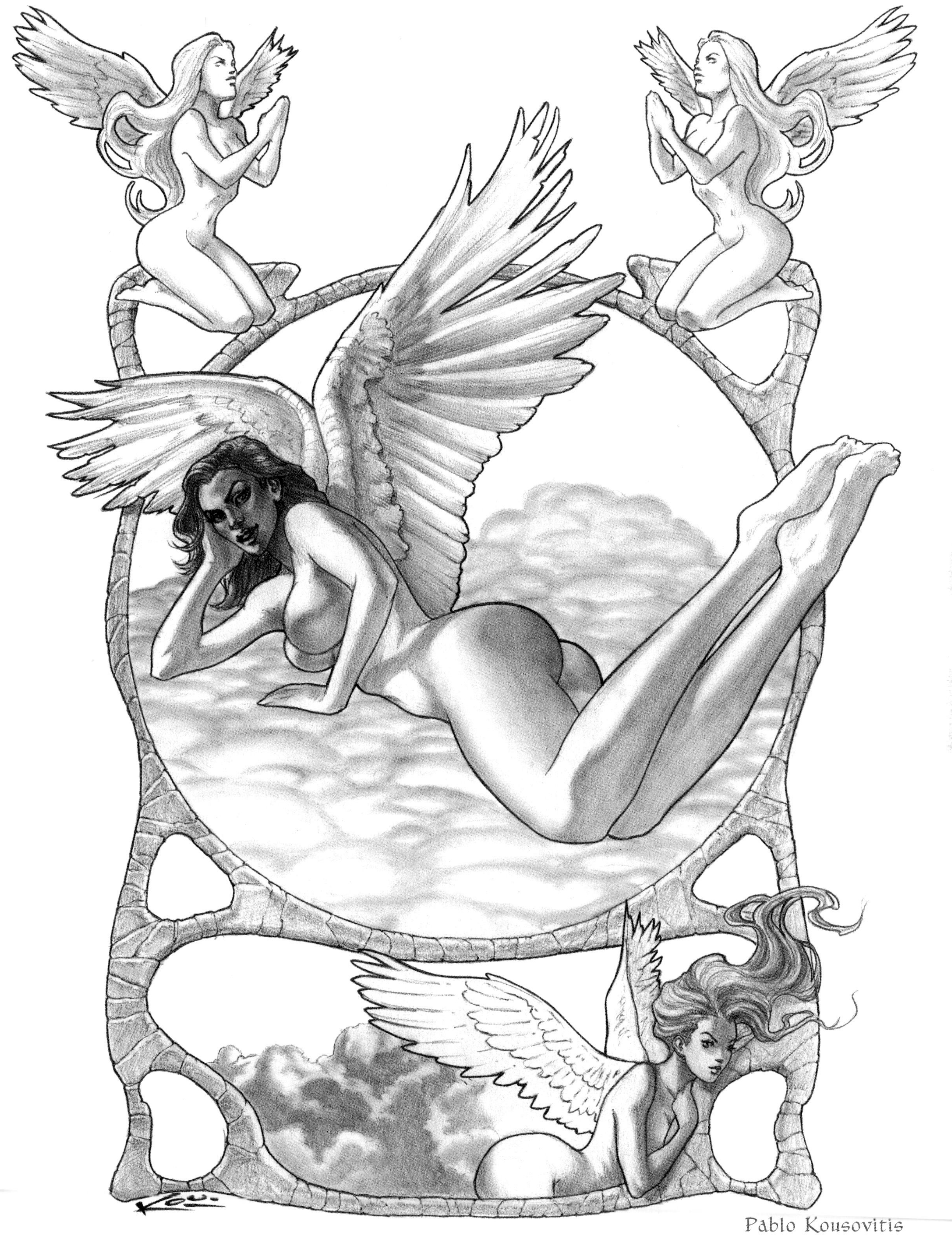

Pablo Kousovitis

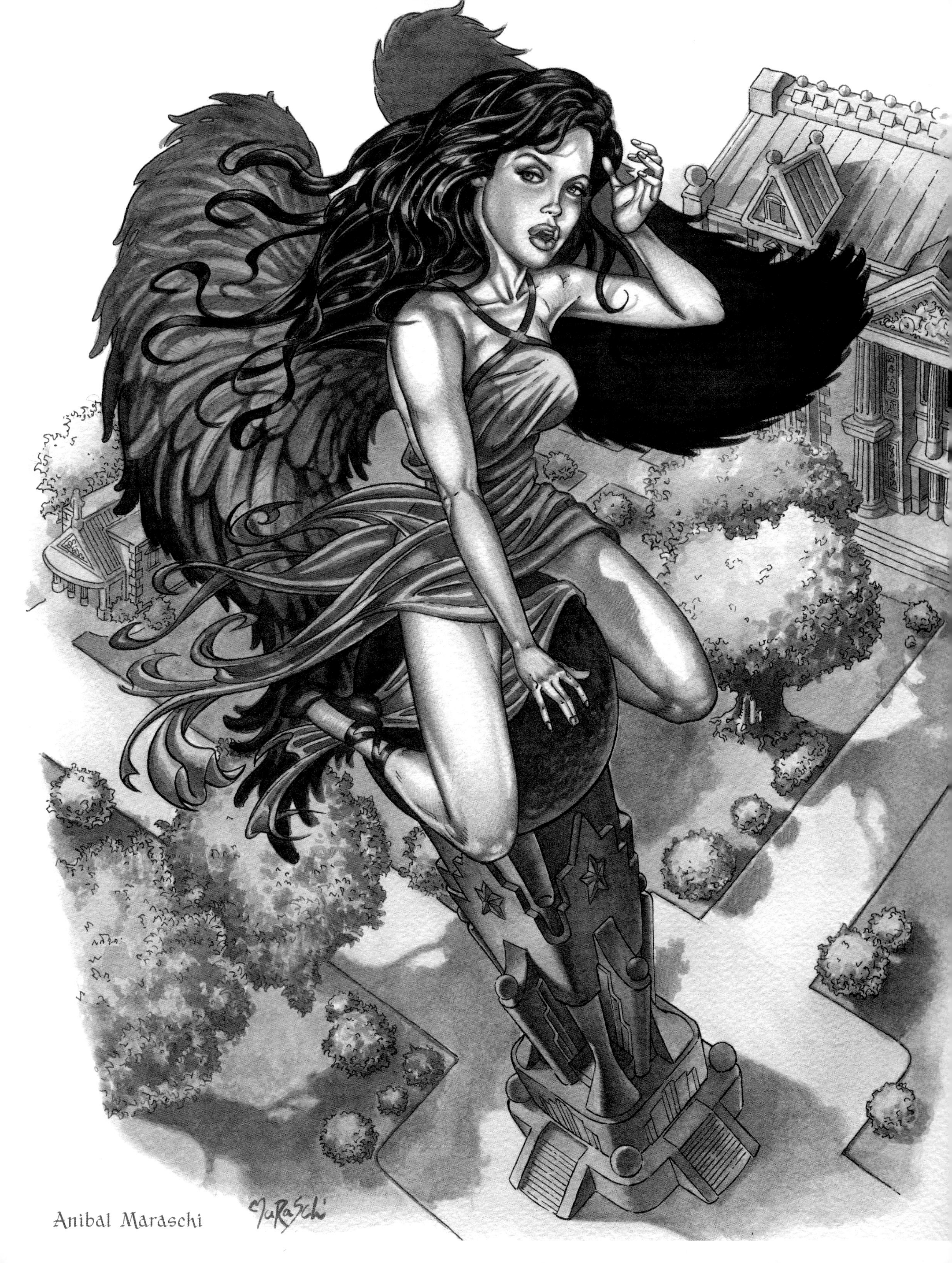

Anibal Maraschi

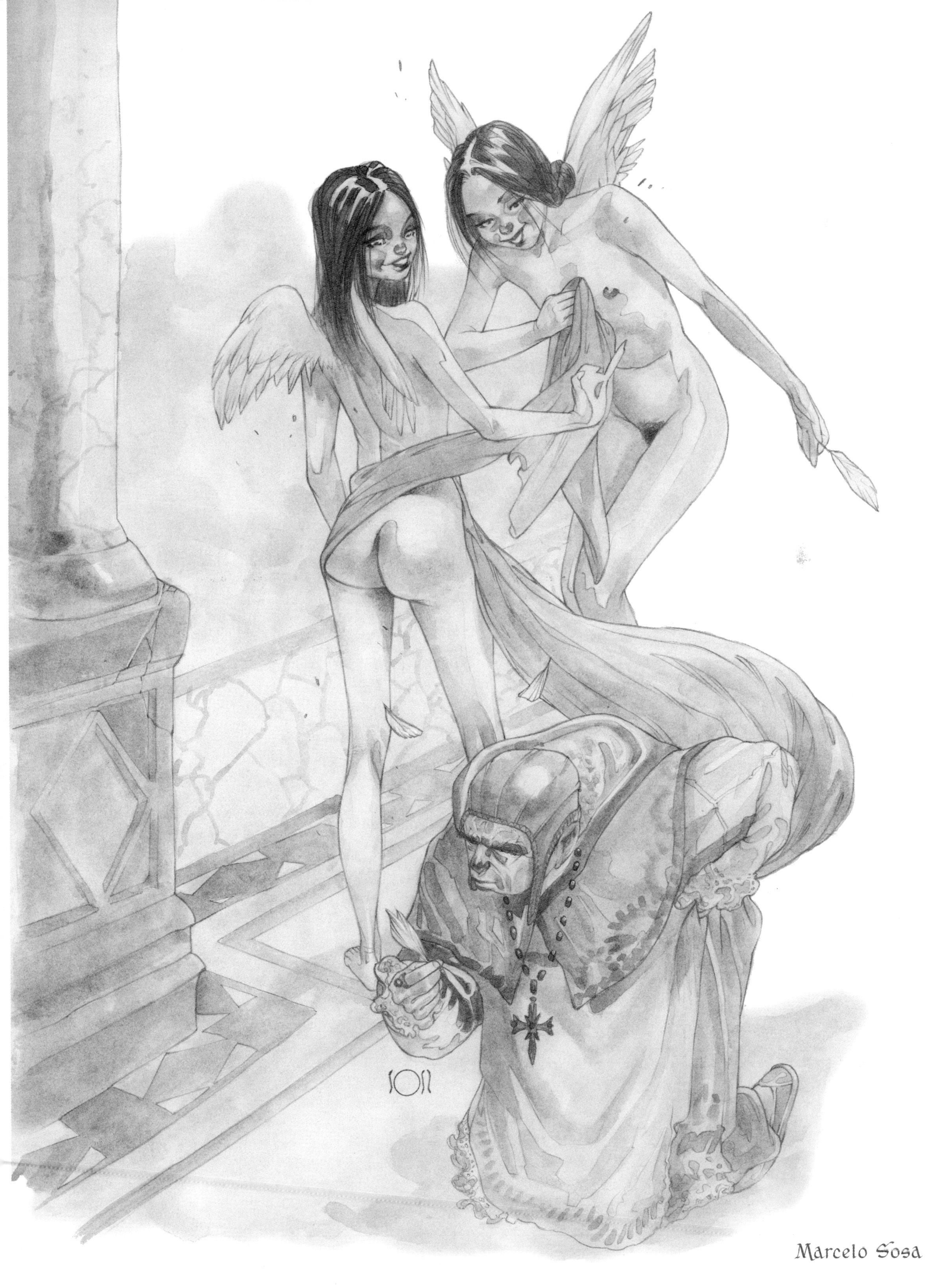

Marcelo Sosa

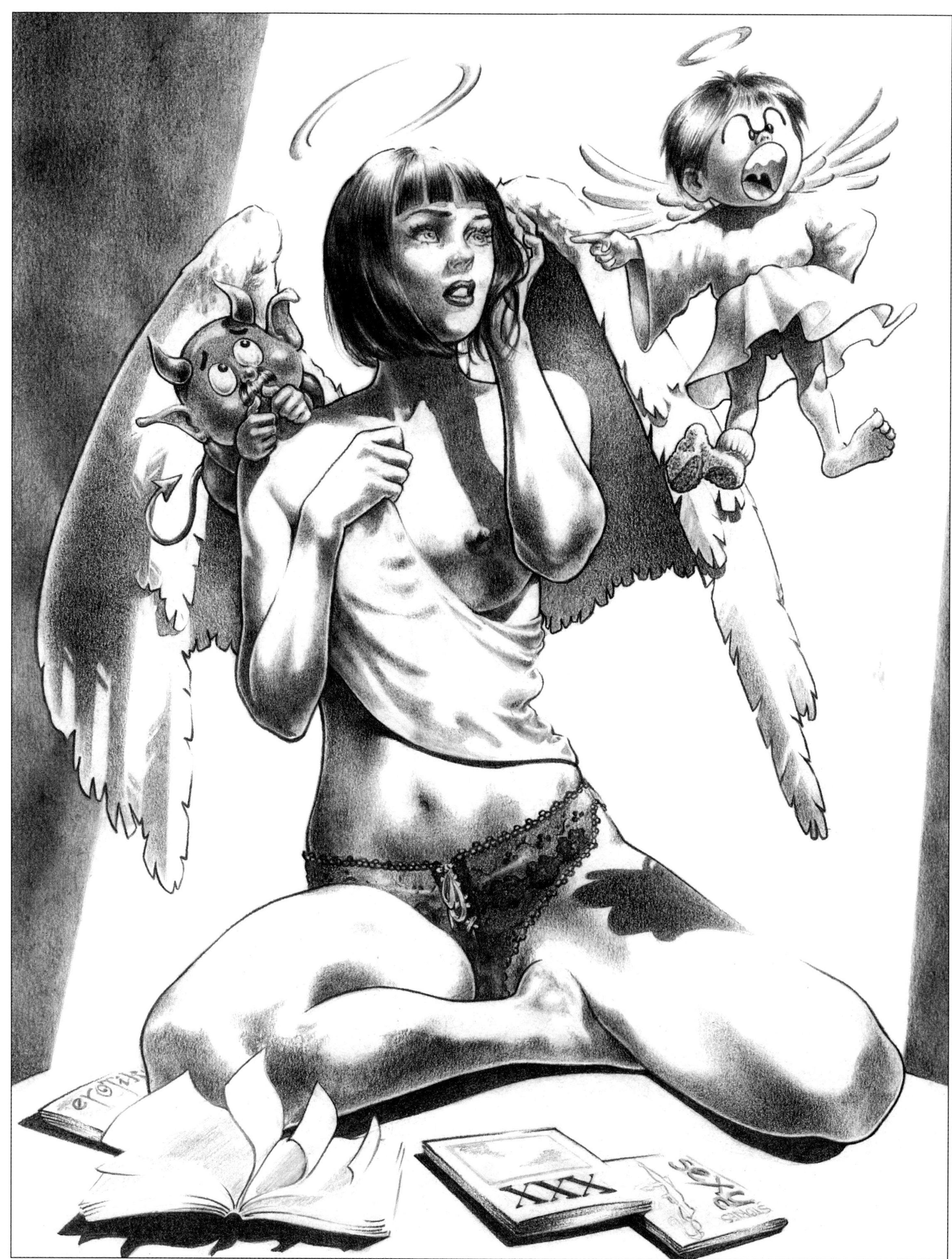

Perla Pilucki

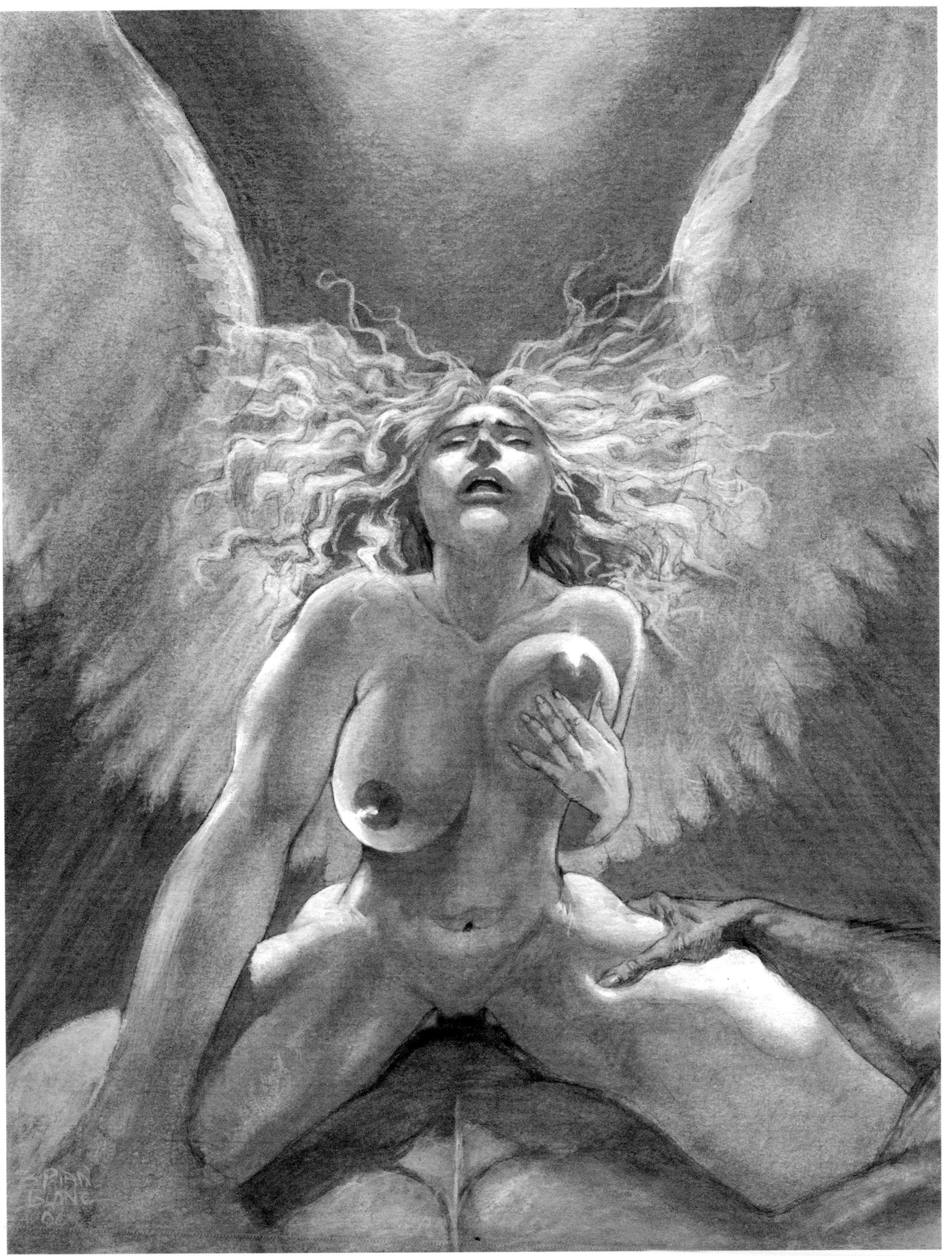

Brian LeBlanc

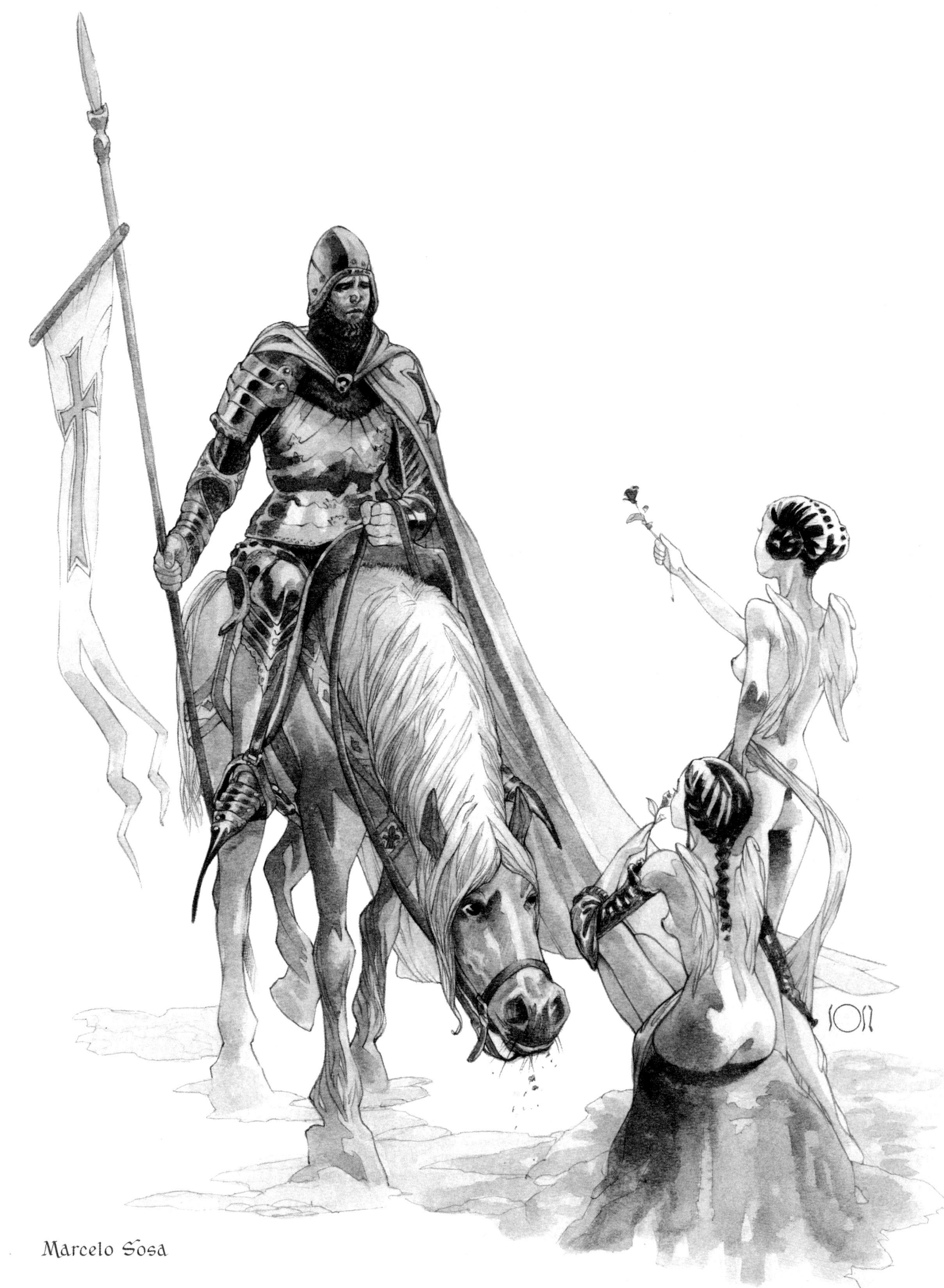

Marcelo Sosa

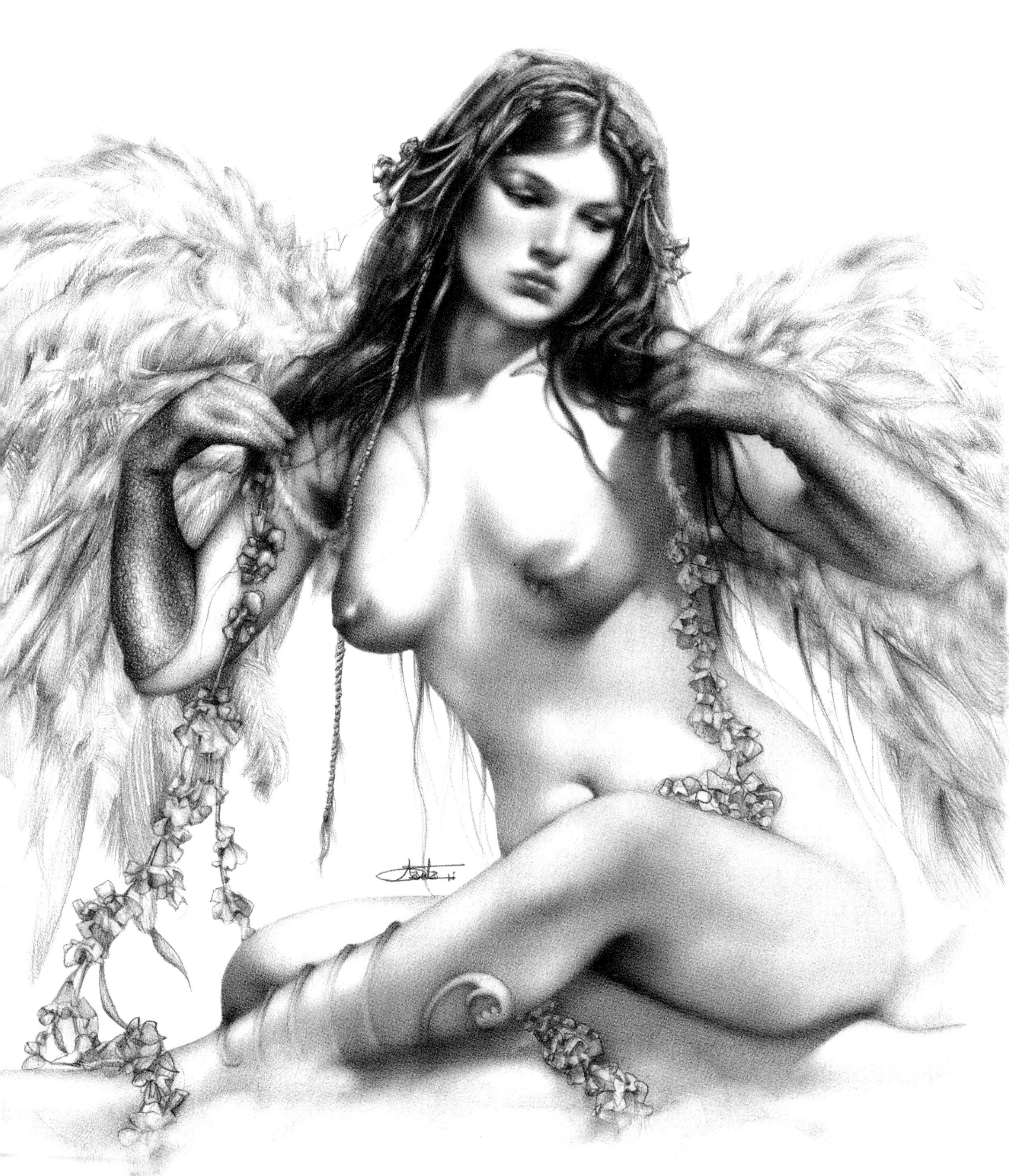

Arantza

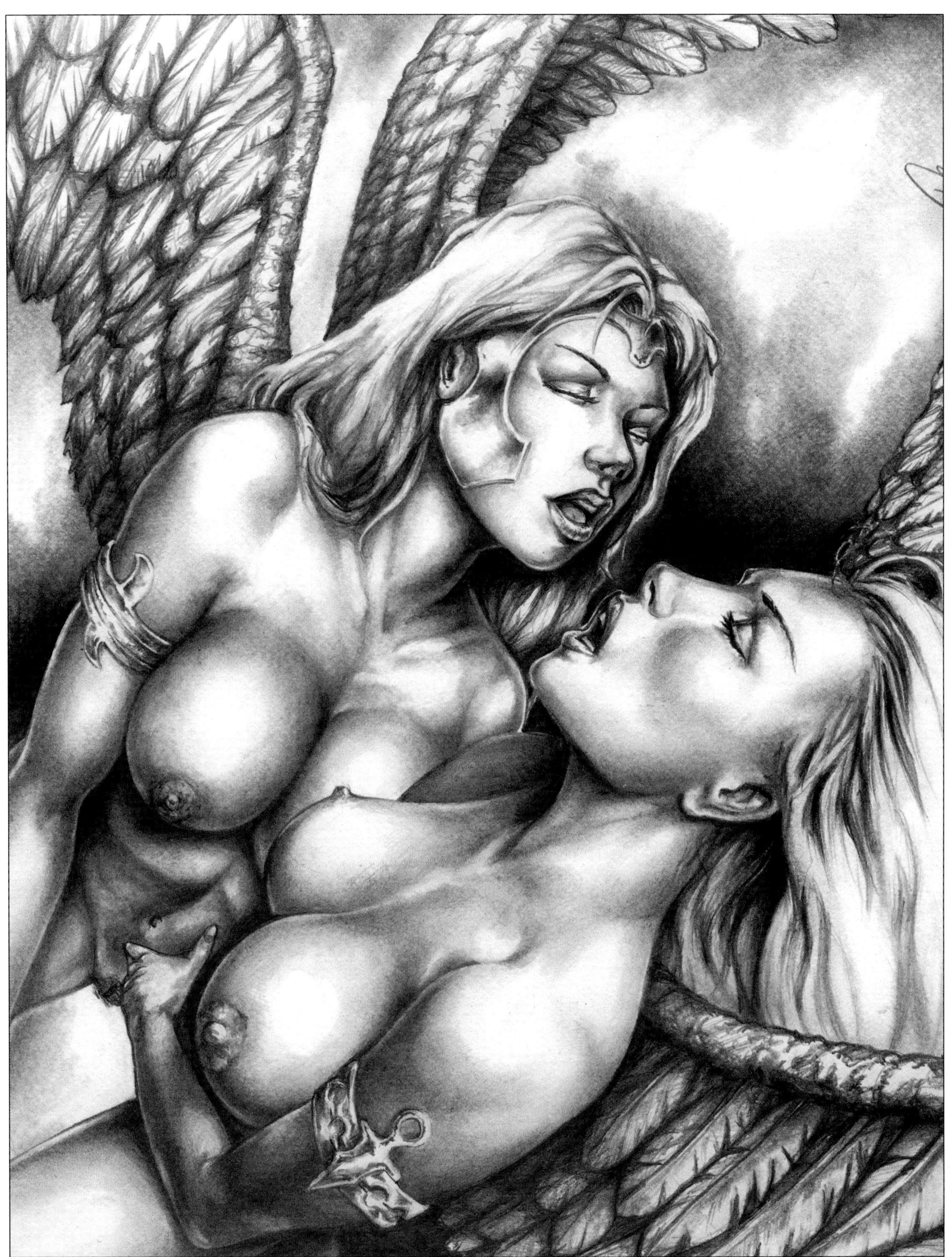

Diego Cândia

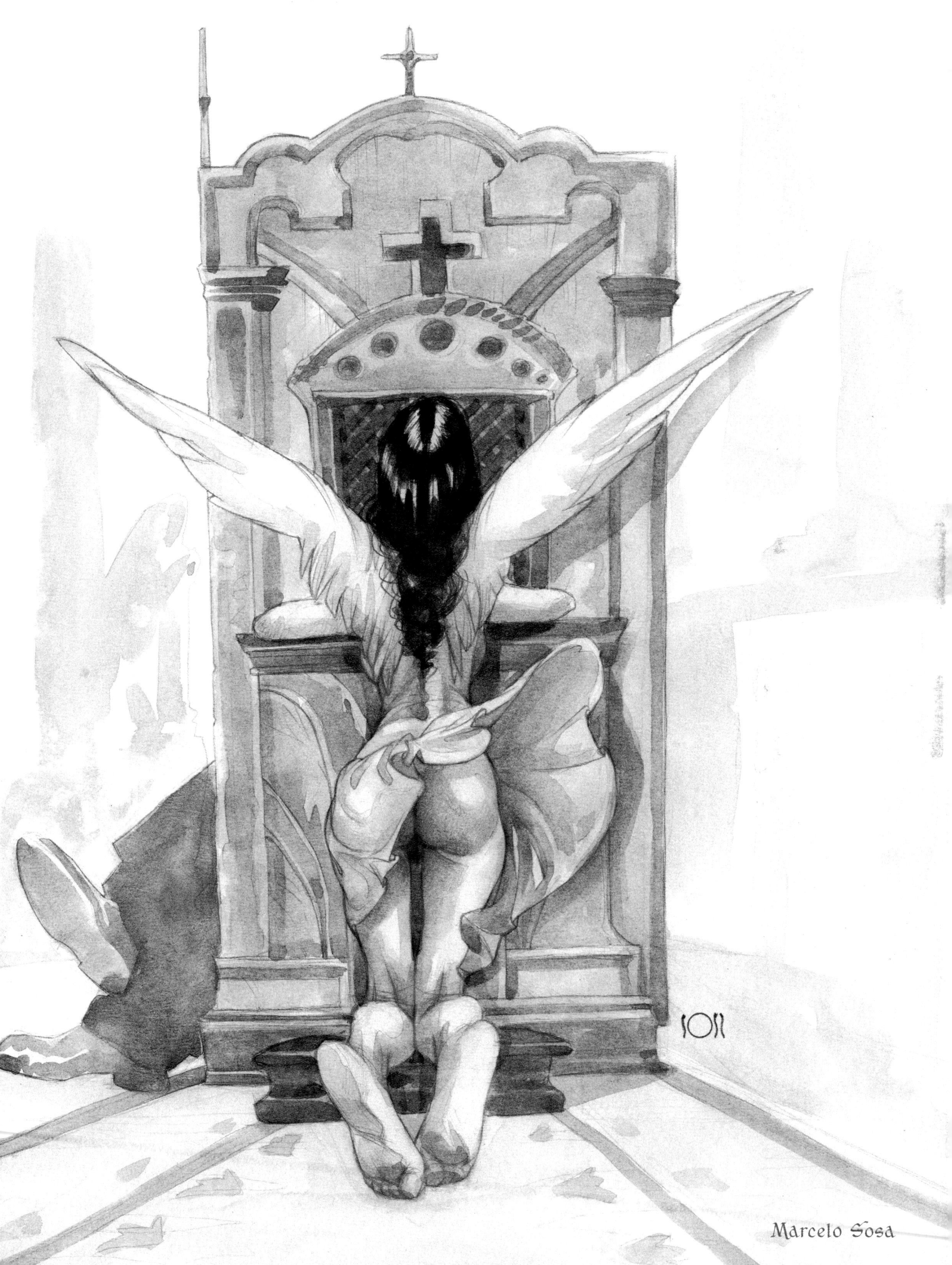

Marcelo Sosa

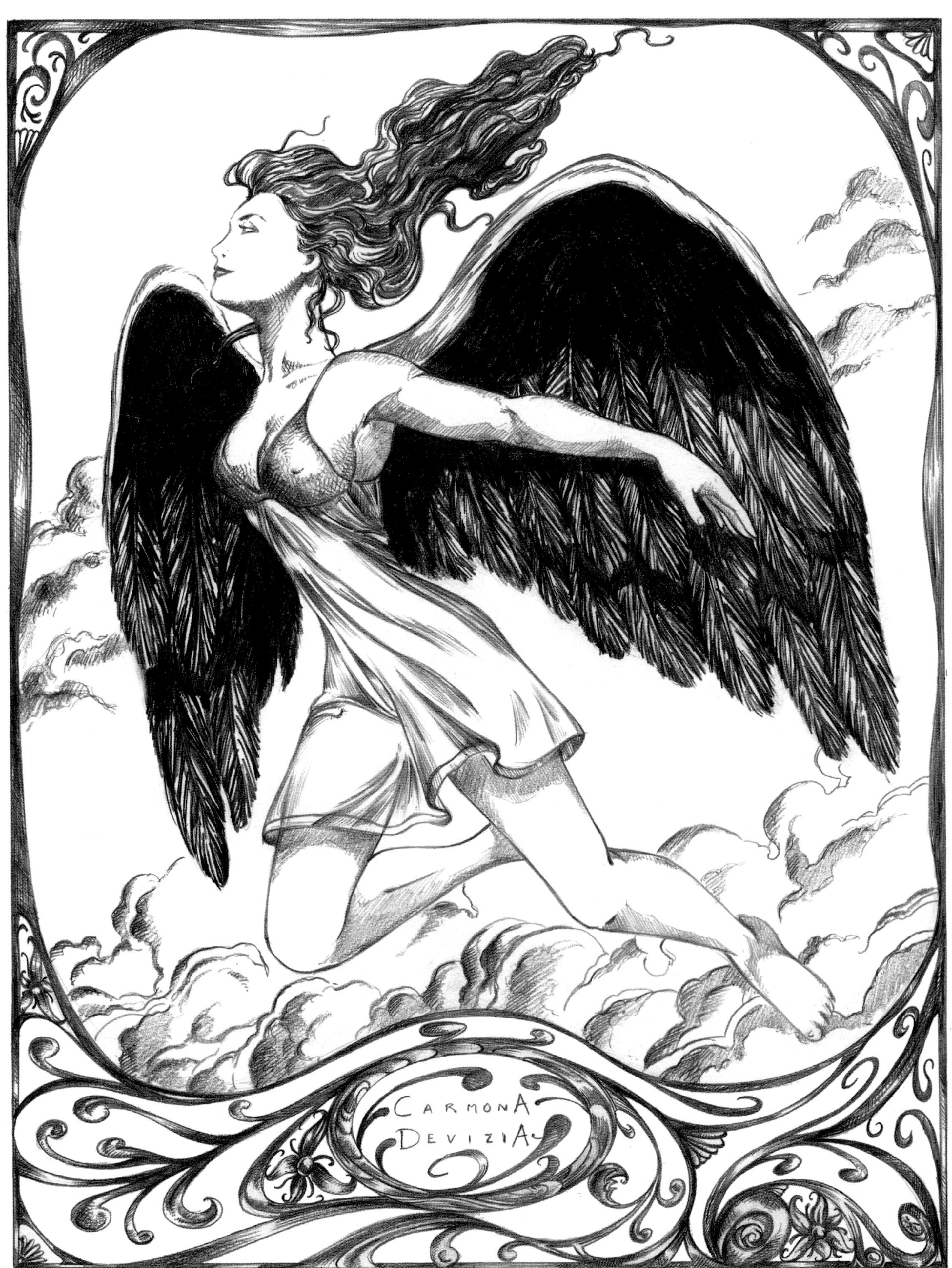

Carmona/Devizia

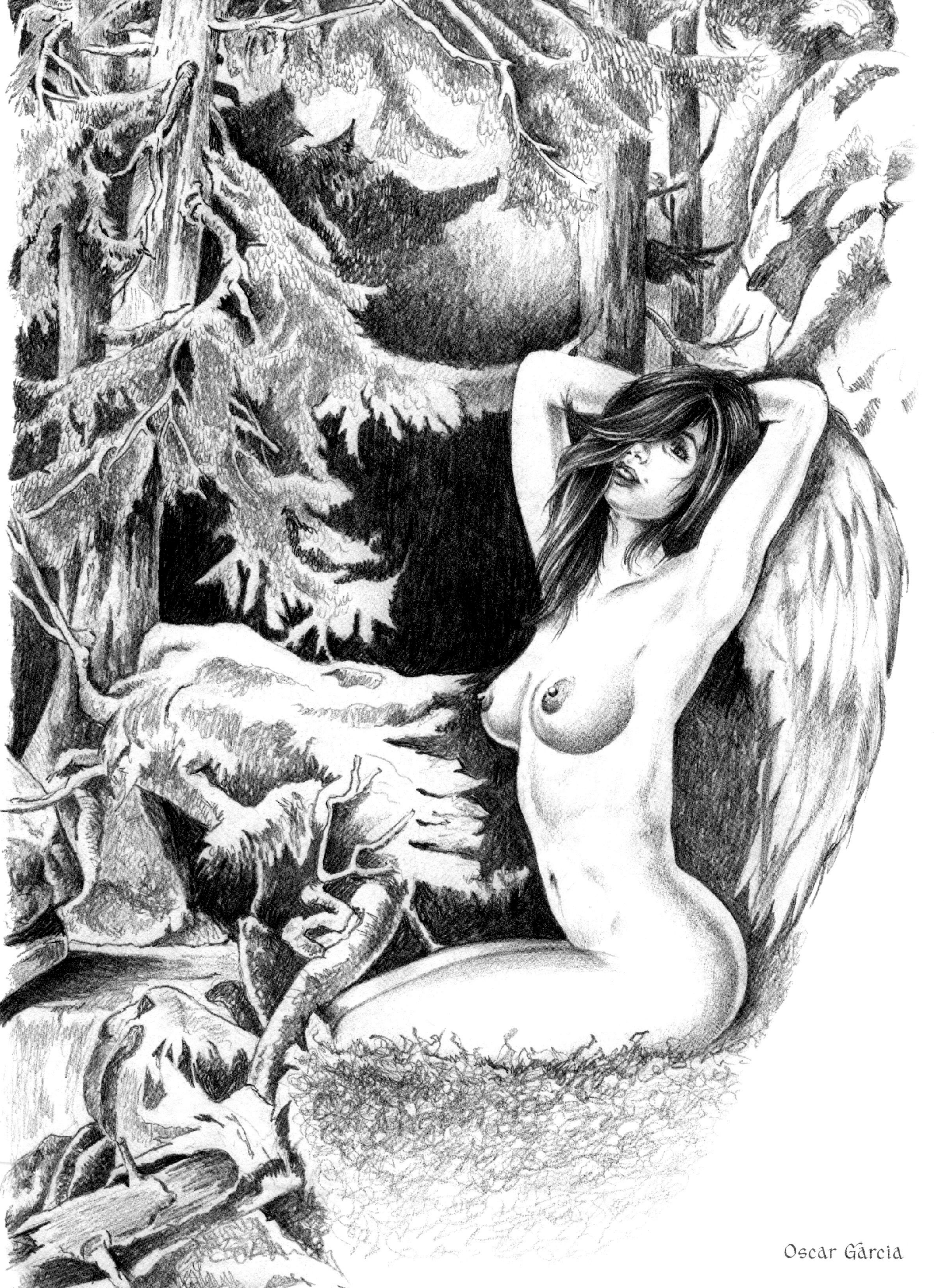
Oscar Gârcia

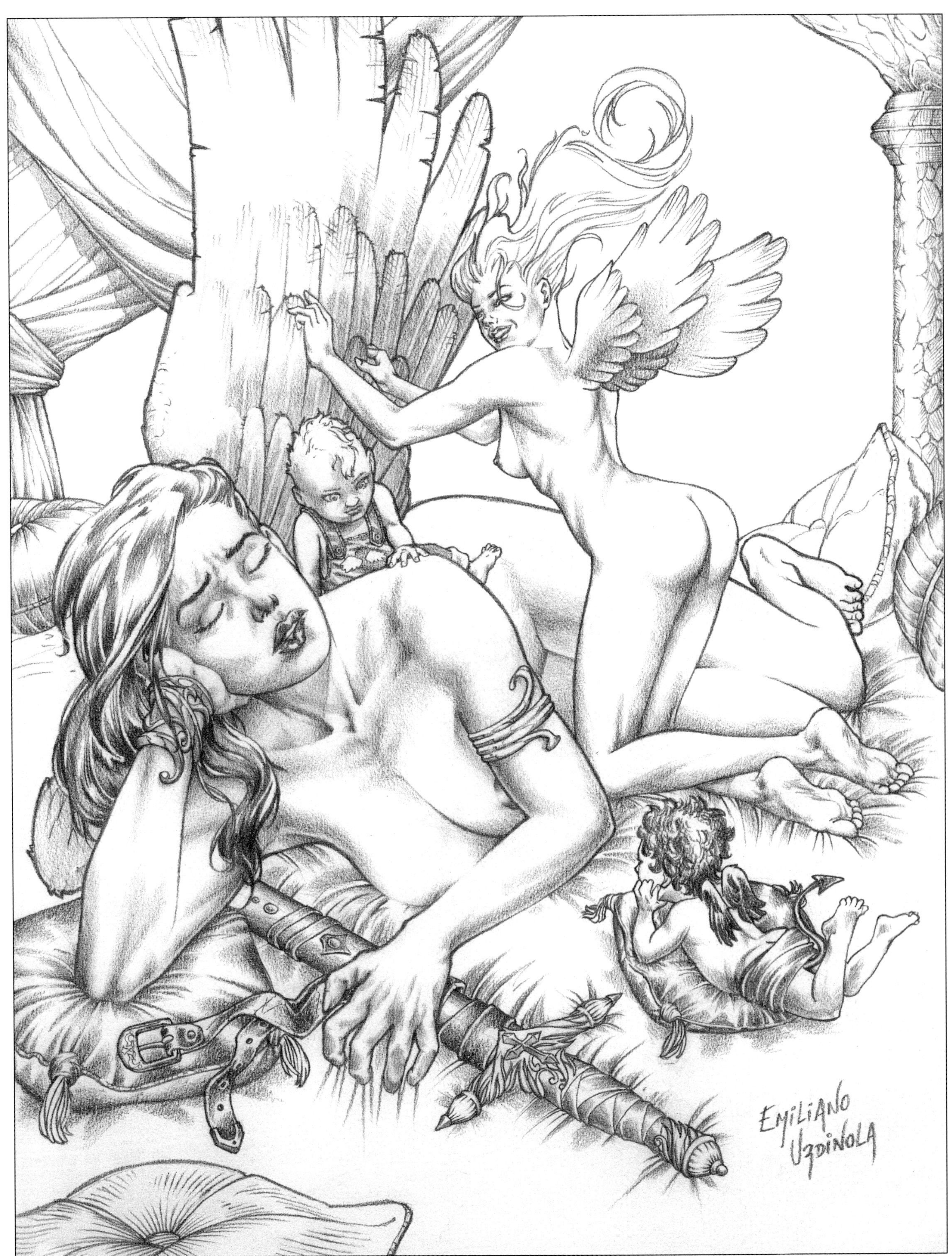

Emiliano Urdinola

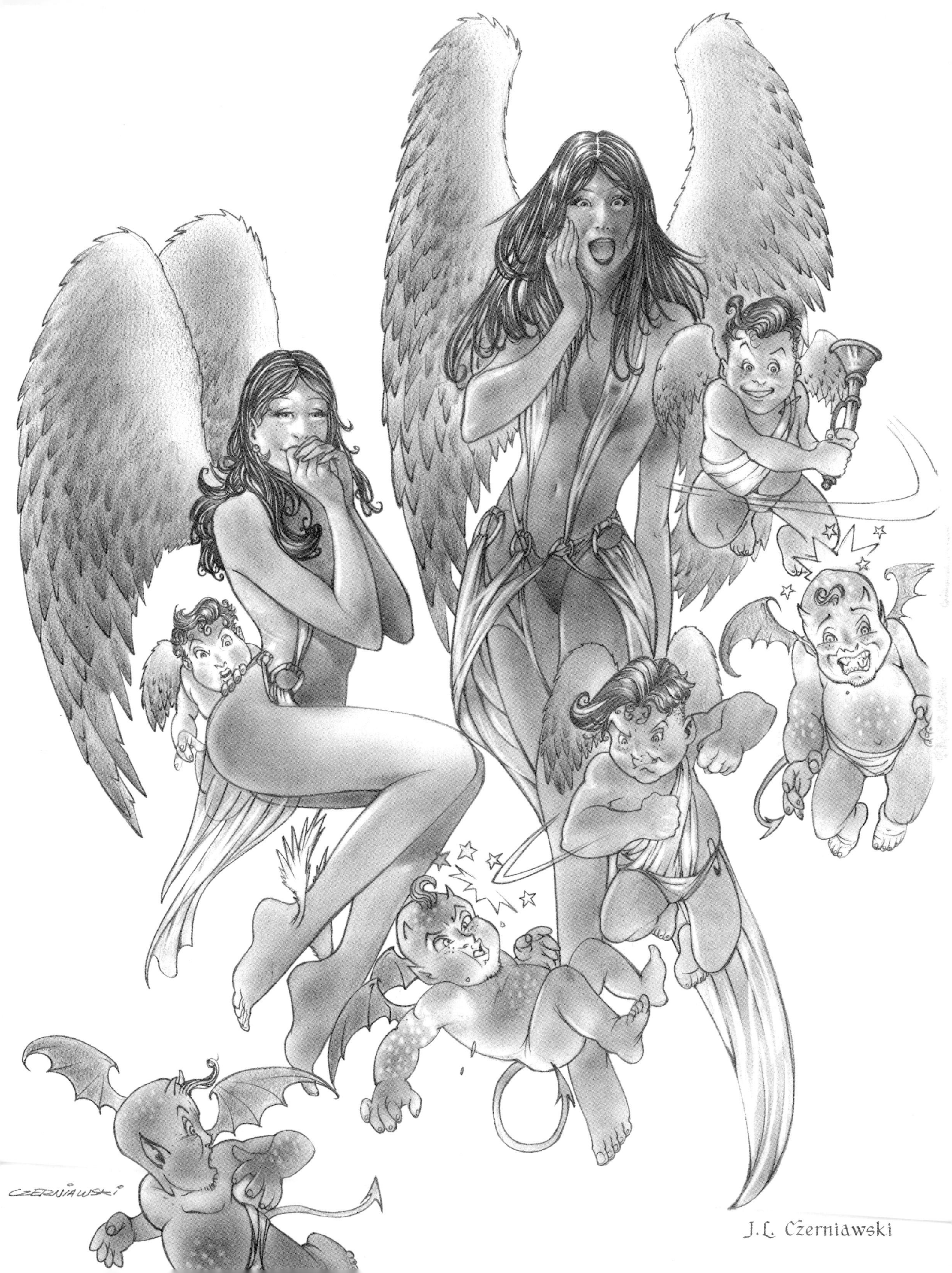
CZERNIAWSKI
J.L. Czerniawski

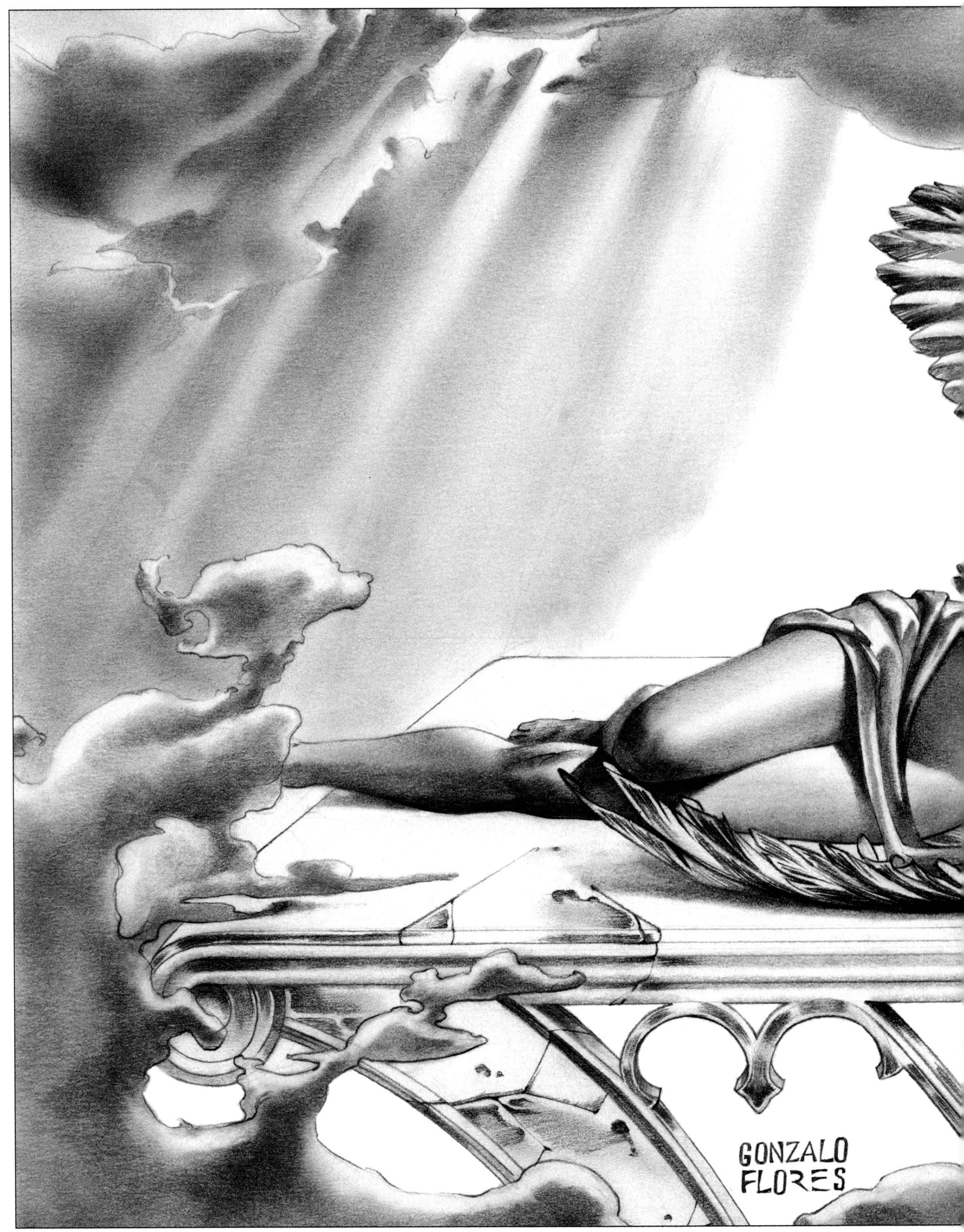
GONZALO
FLORES

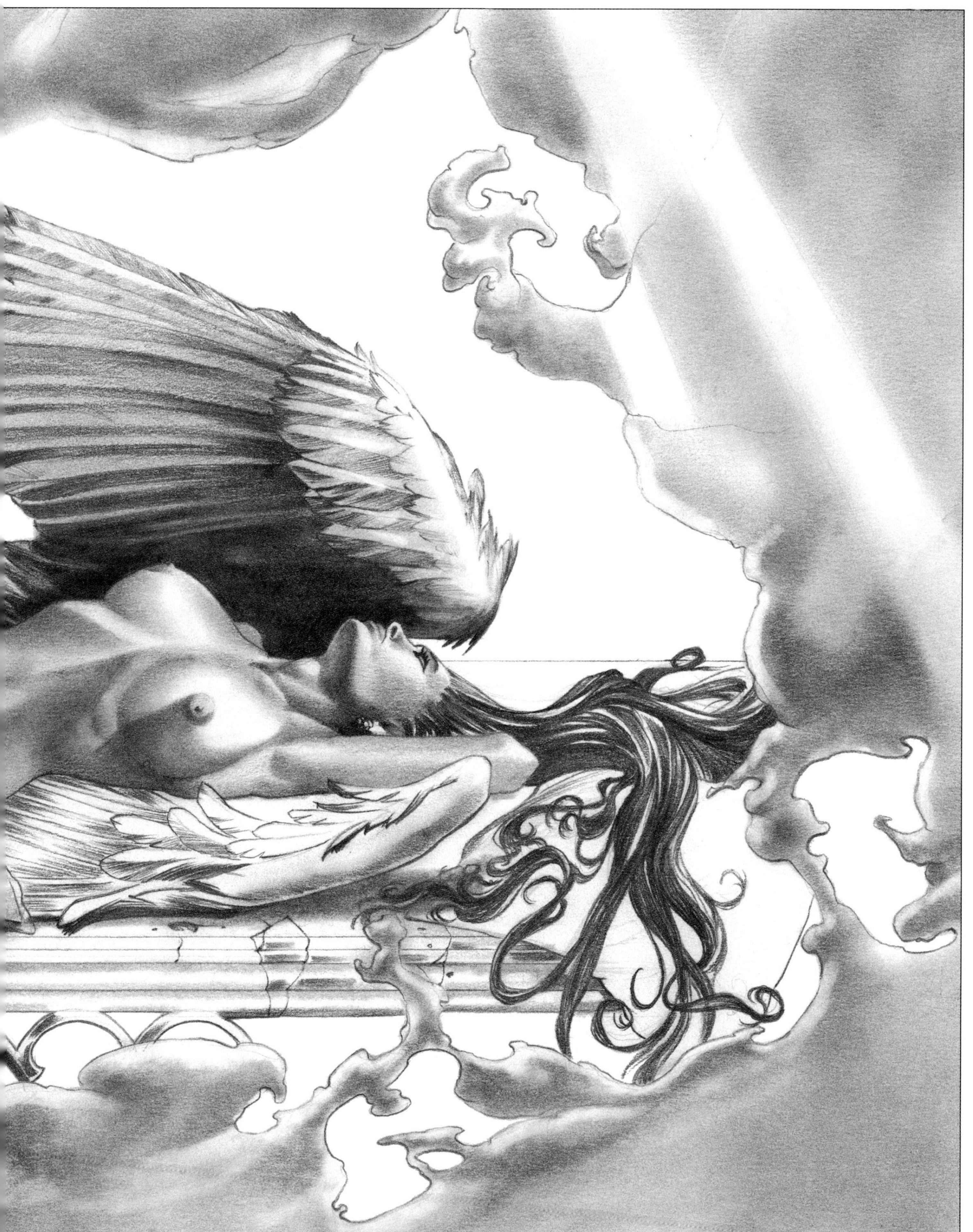

Gonzalo Flores

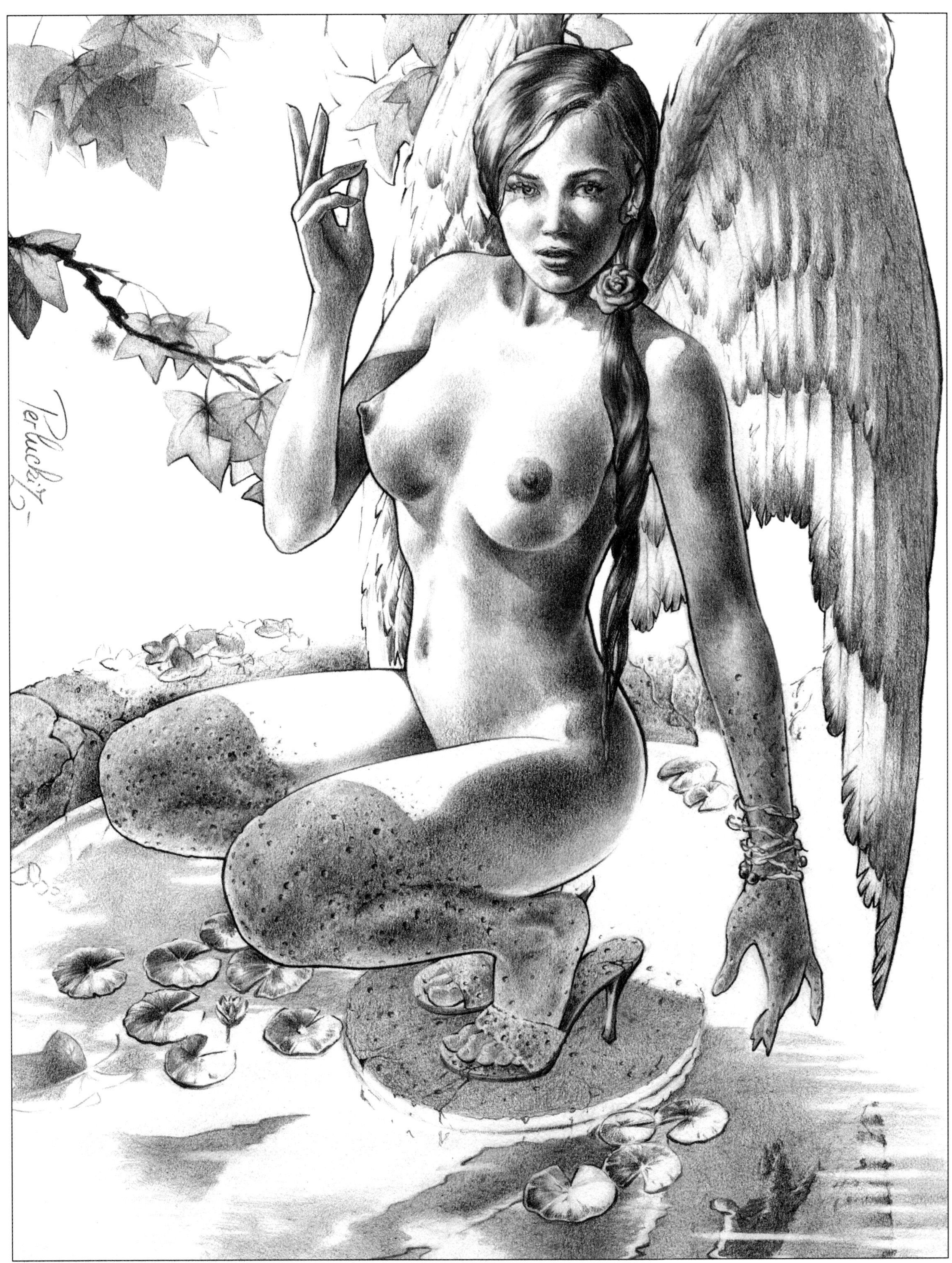

Perla Pilucki

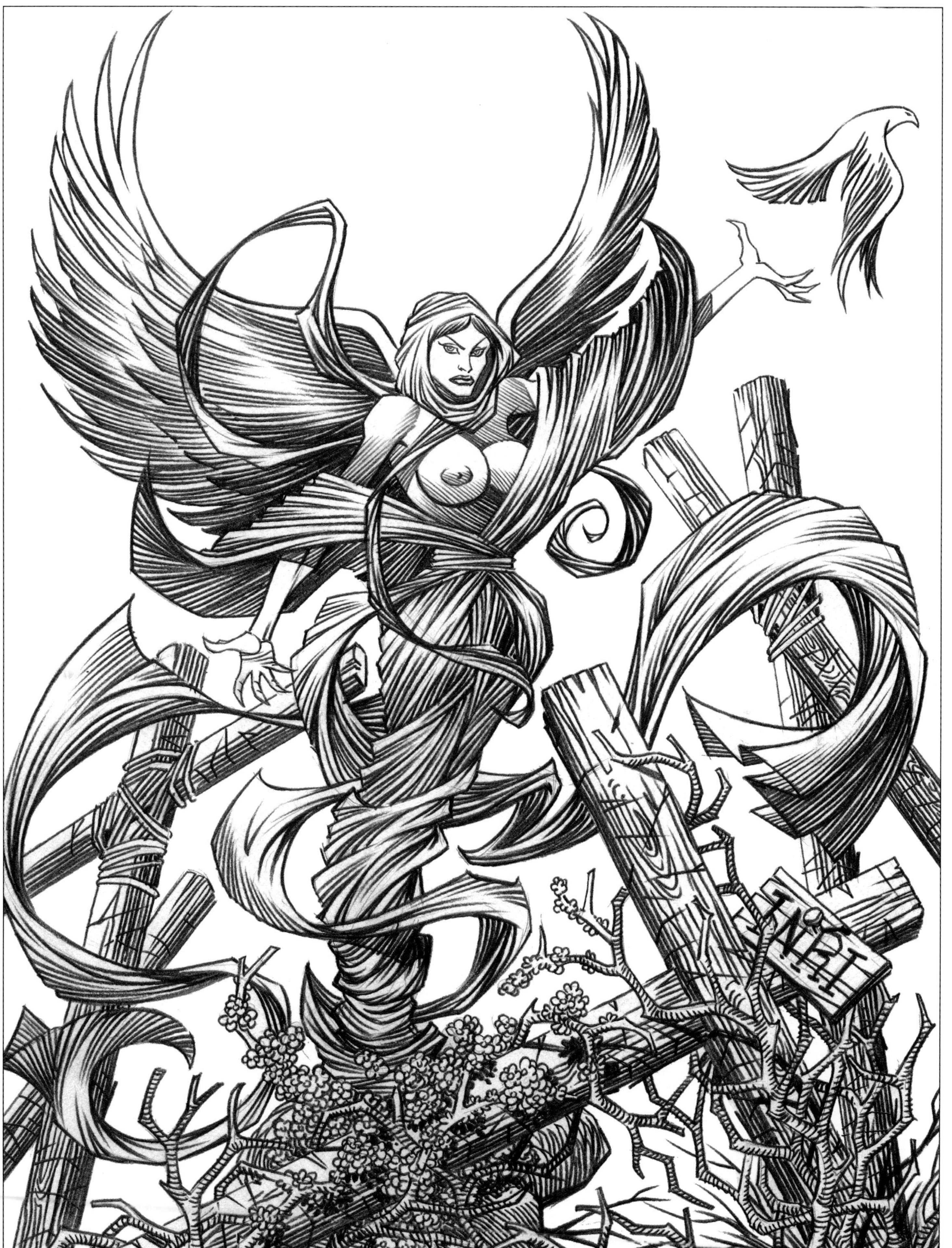

Ruben Meriggi

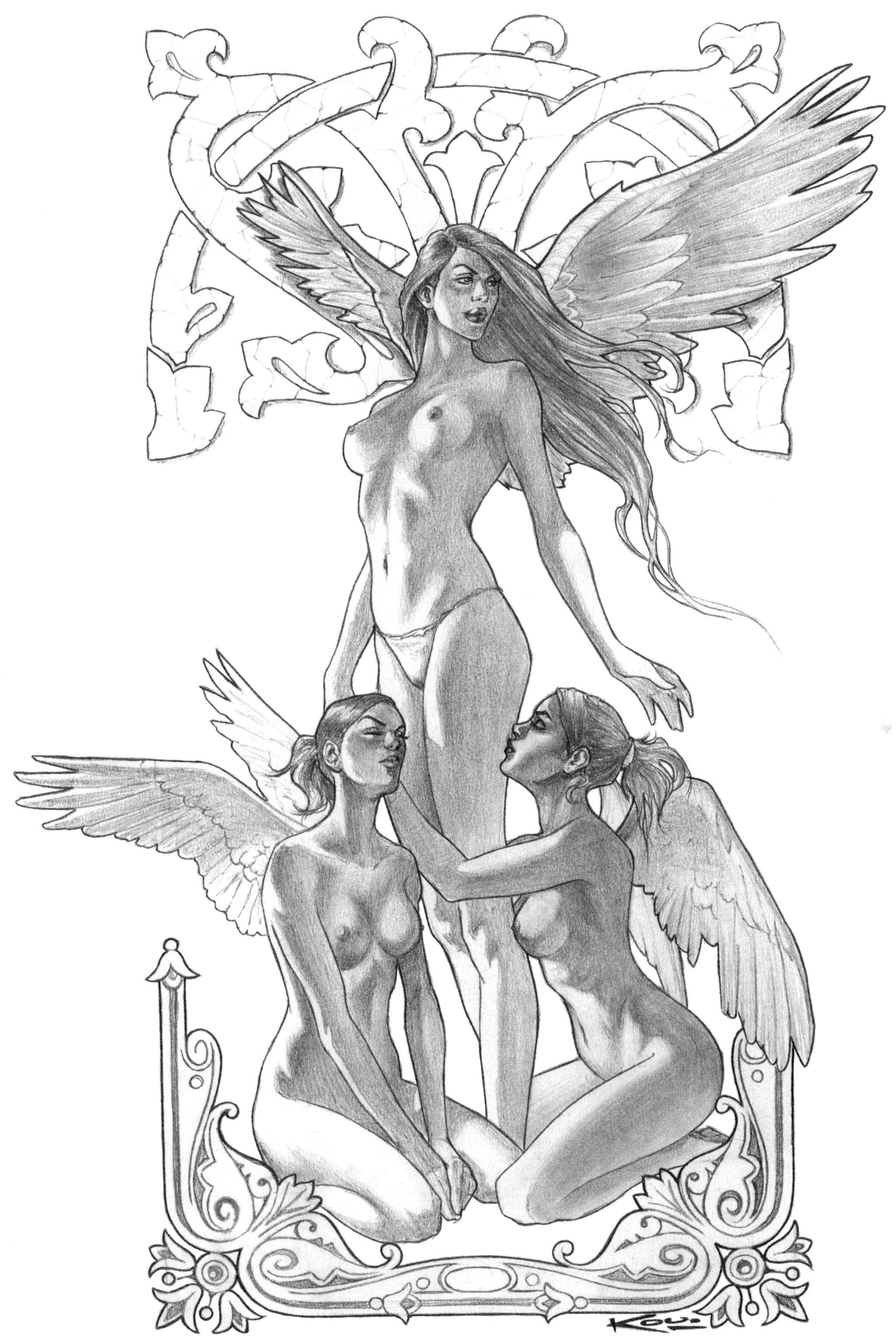

Pablo Kousovitis

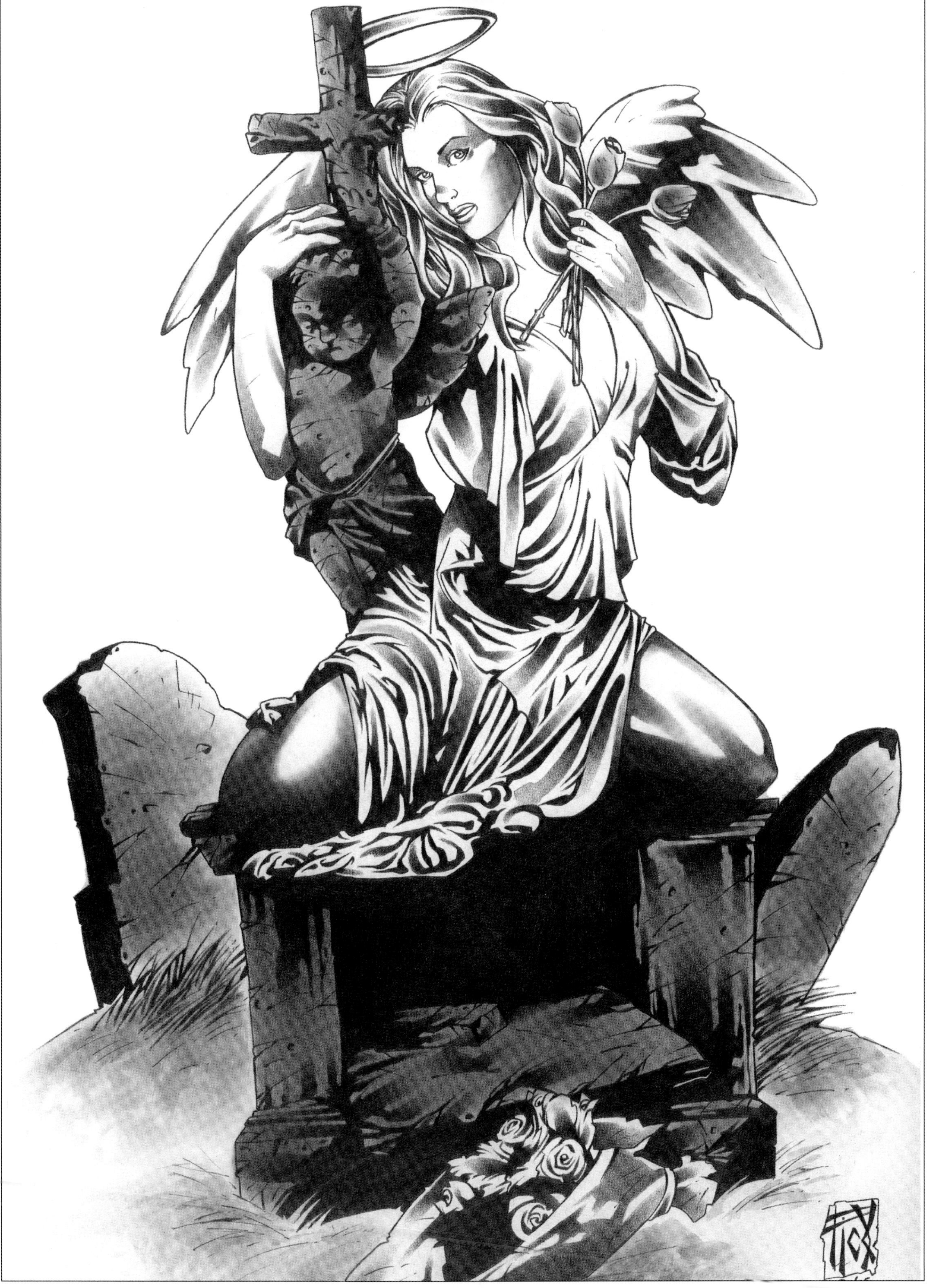

Federico Ossio

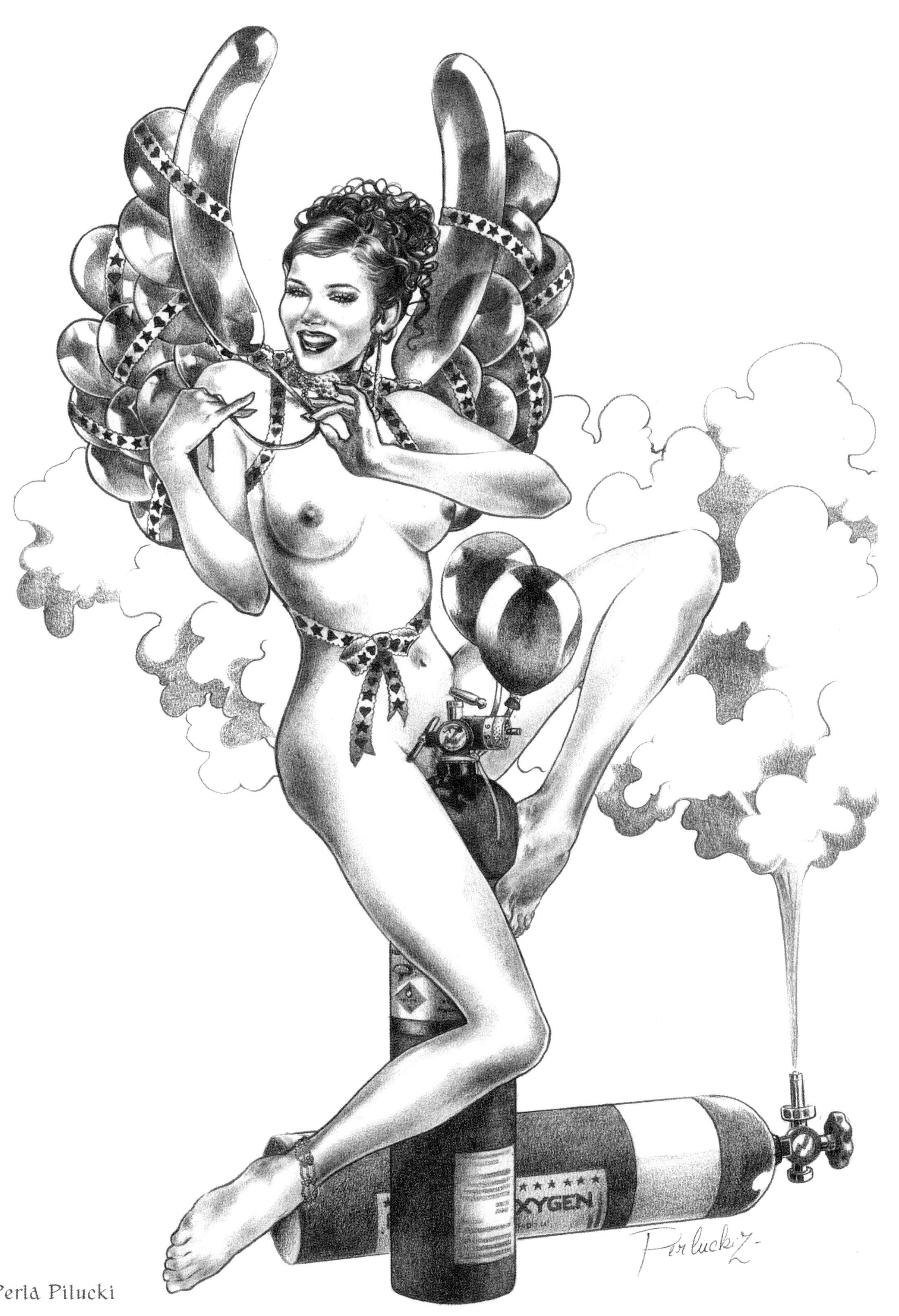

Perla Pilucki

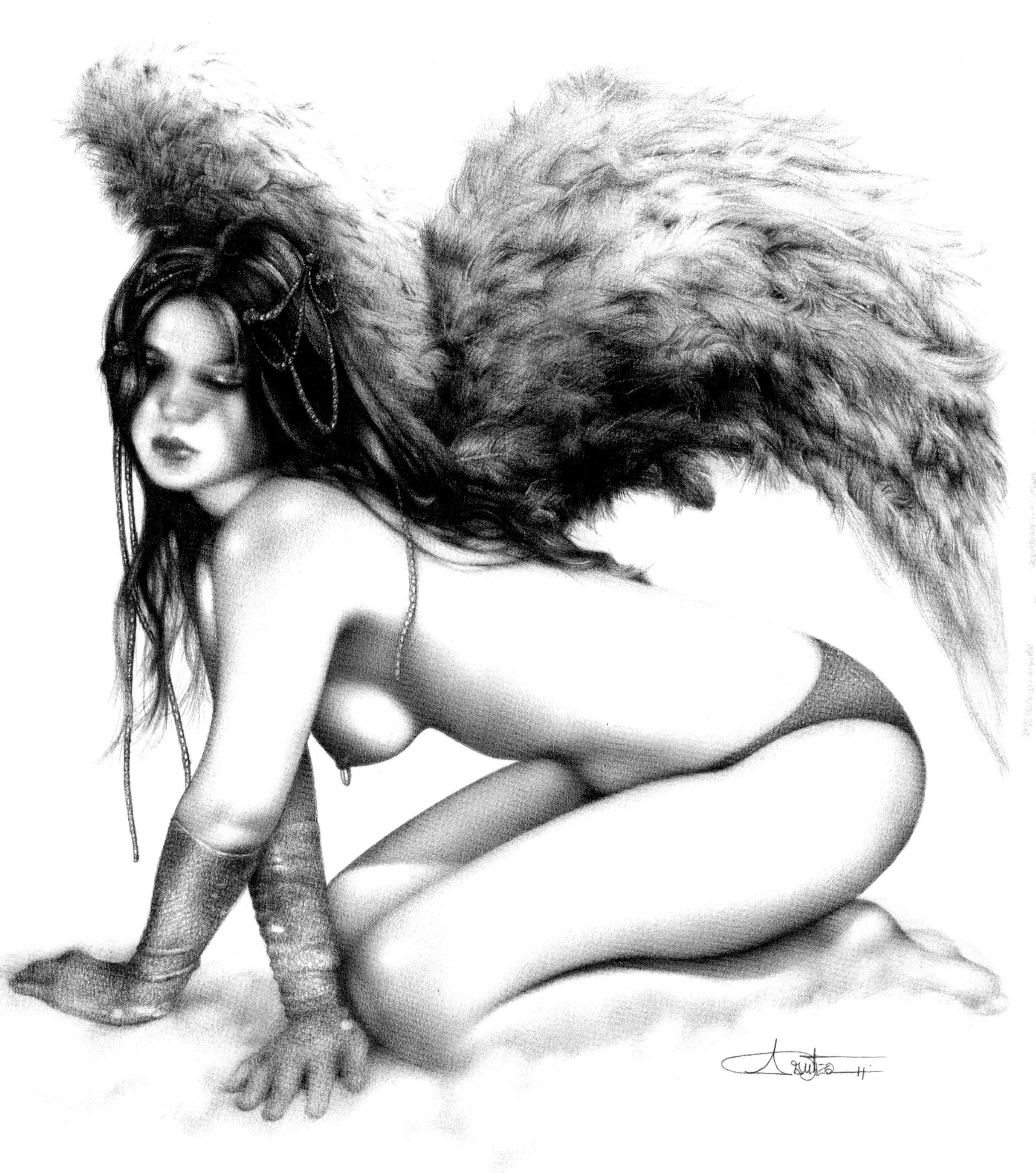

Arantza

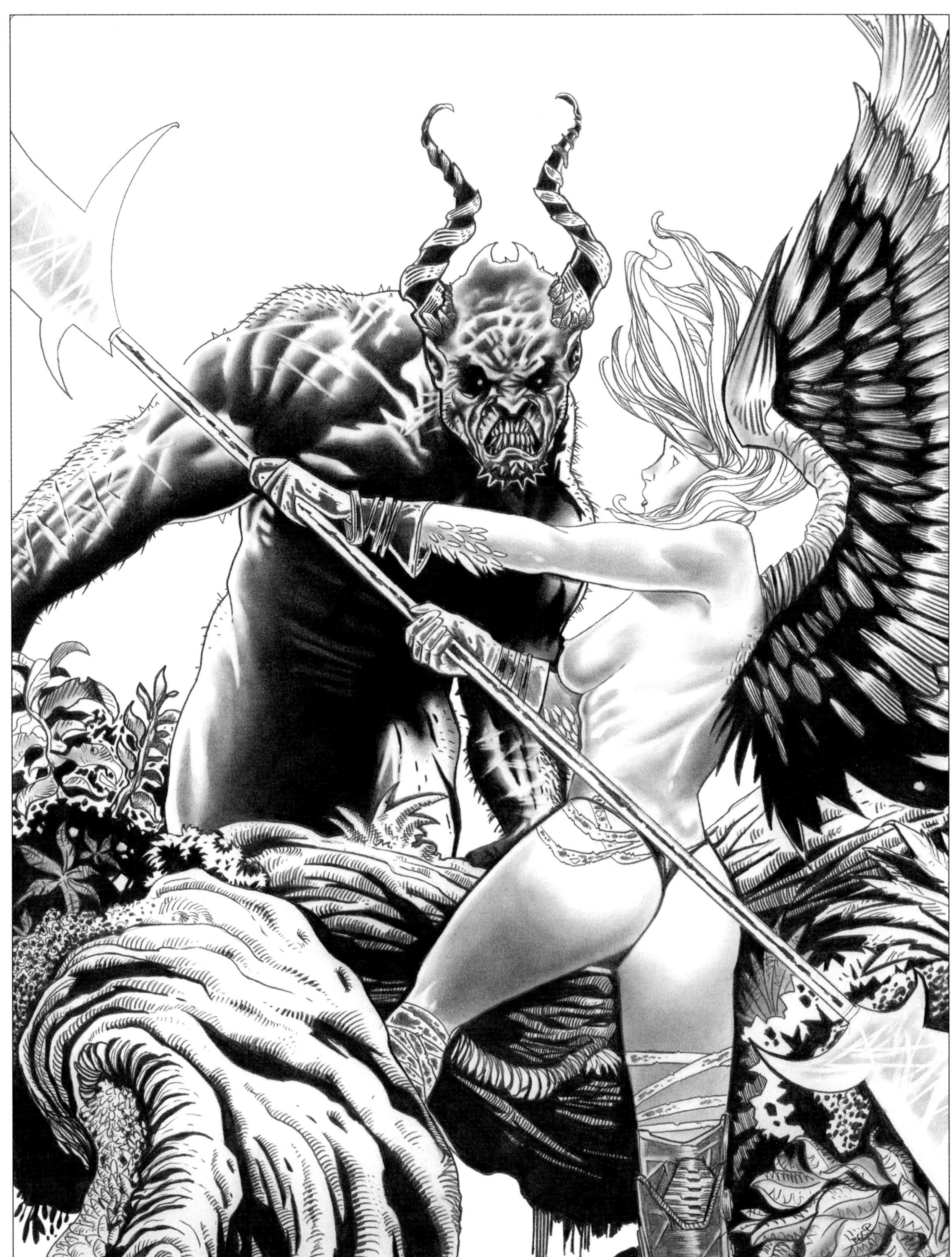

Luis Buci

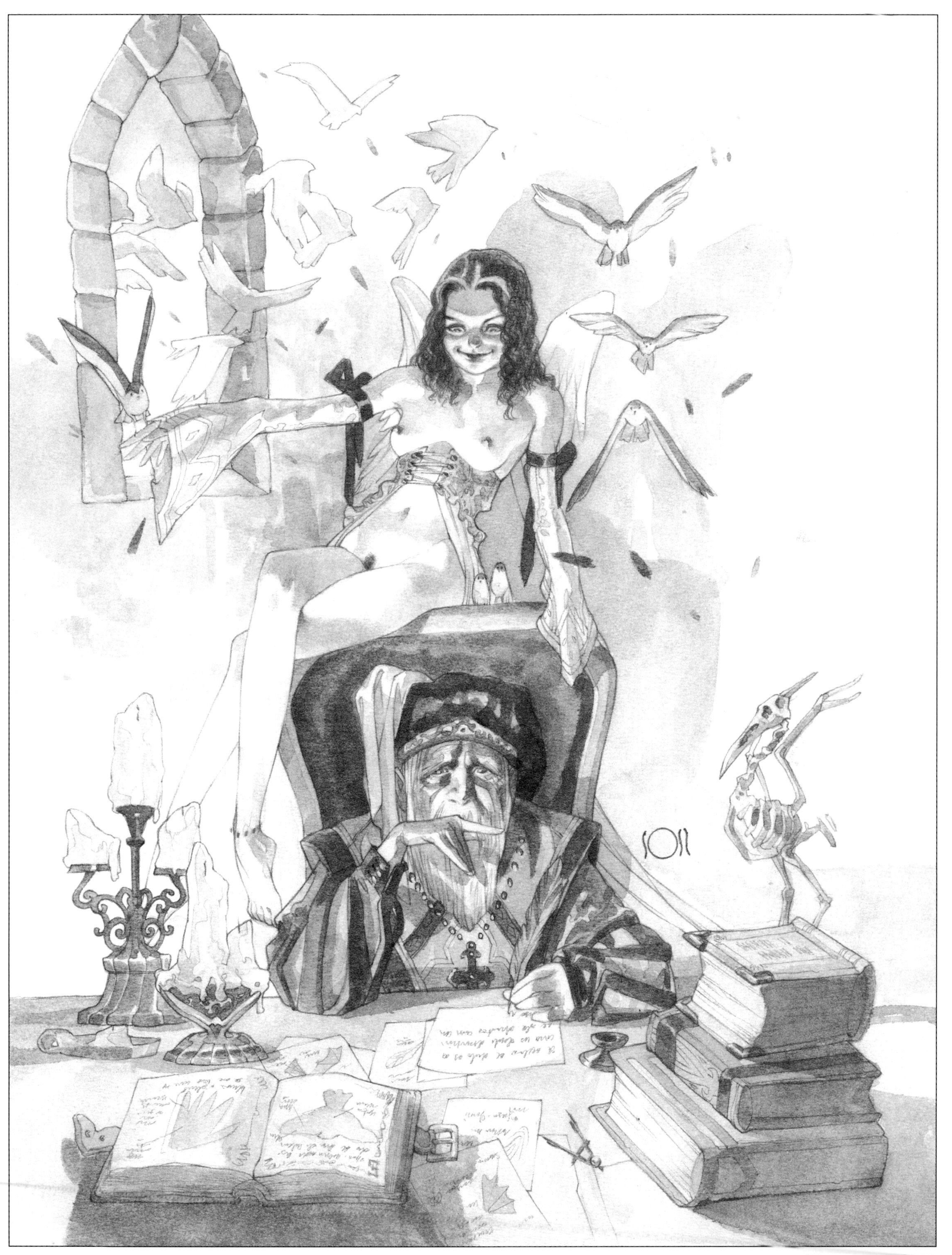

Marcelo Sosa

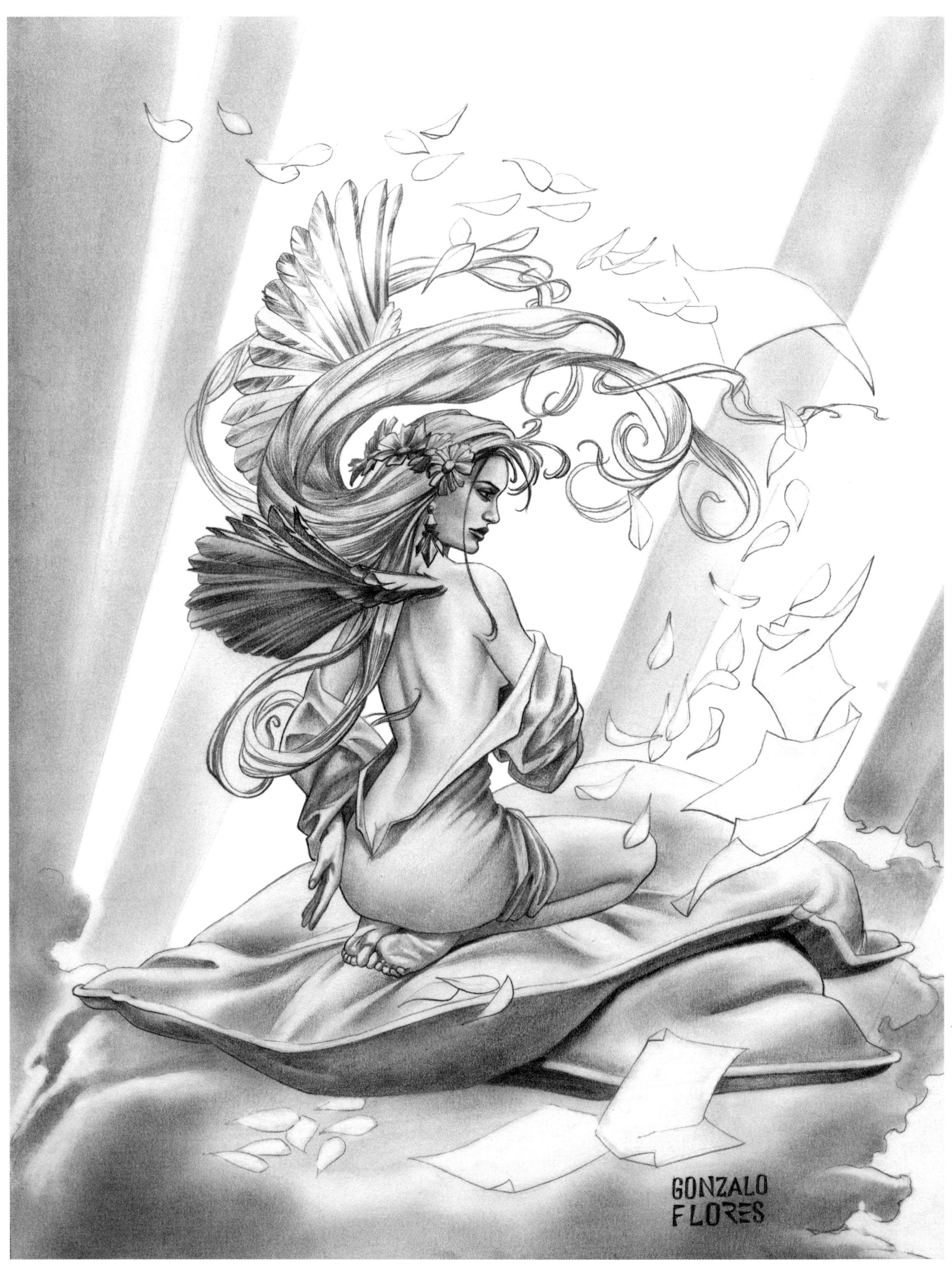

Gonzalo Flores

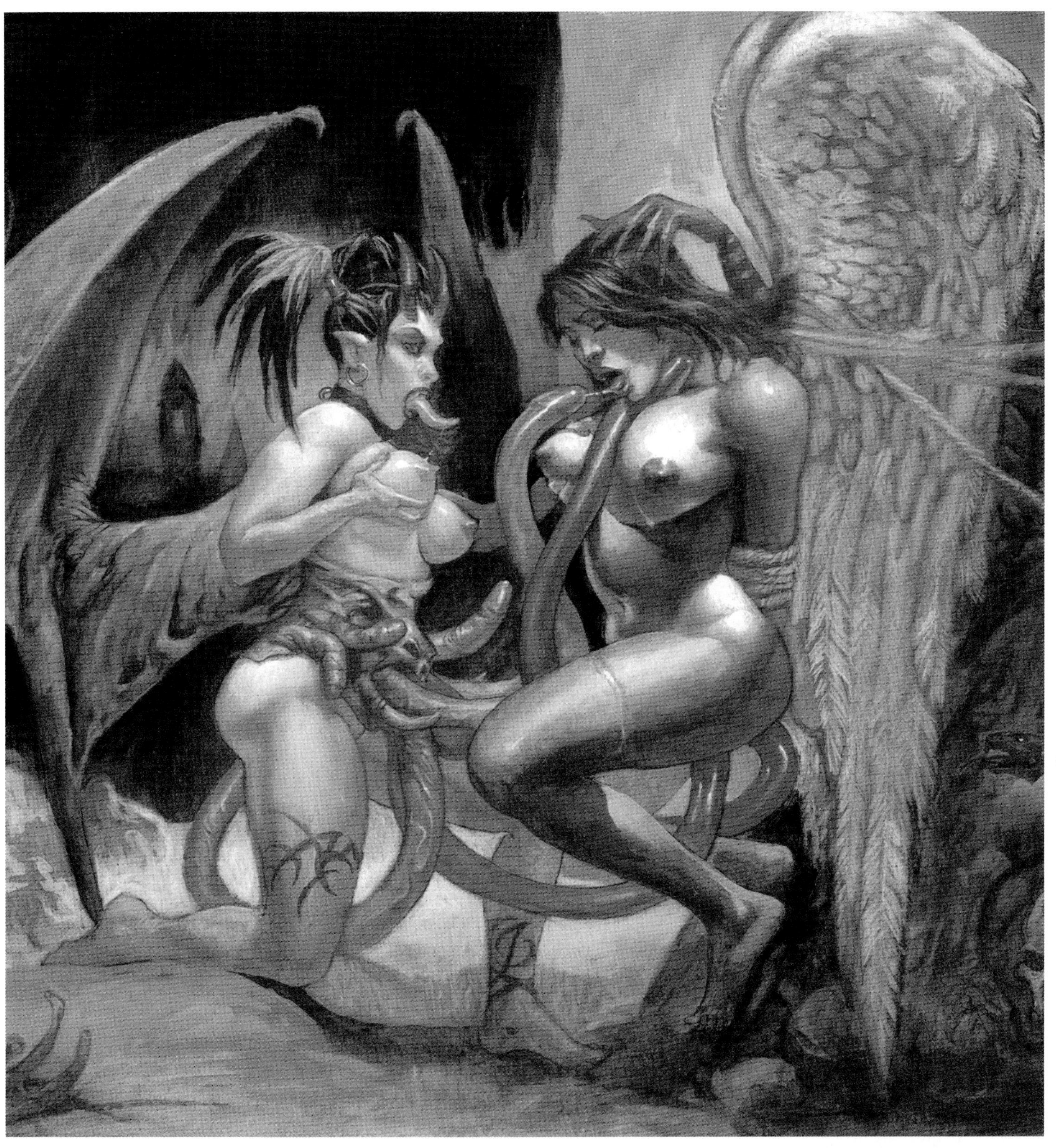

Brian LeBlanc

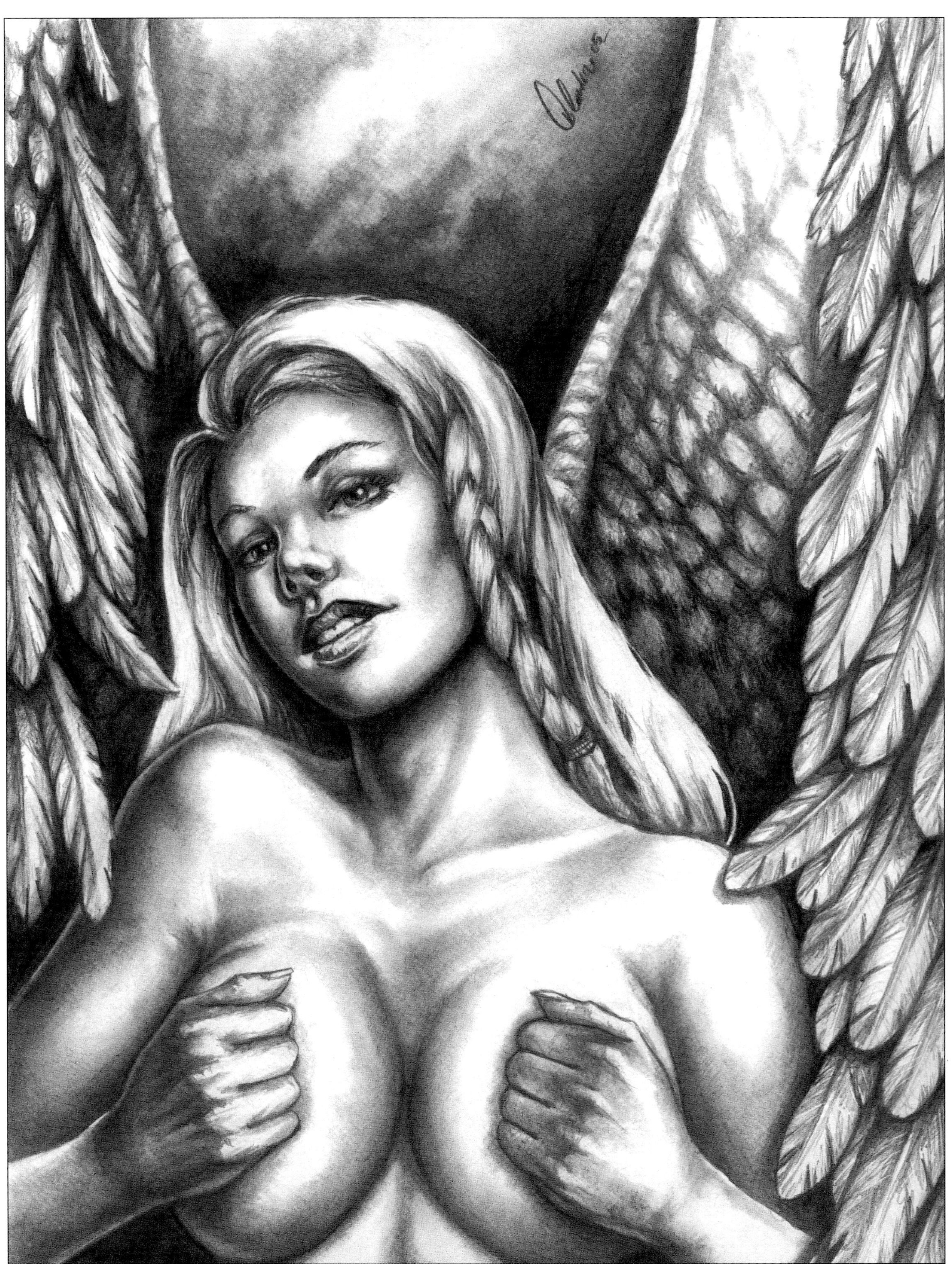

Diego Cândia

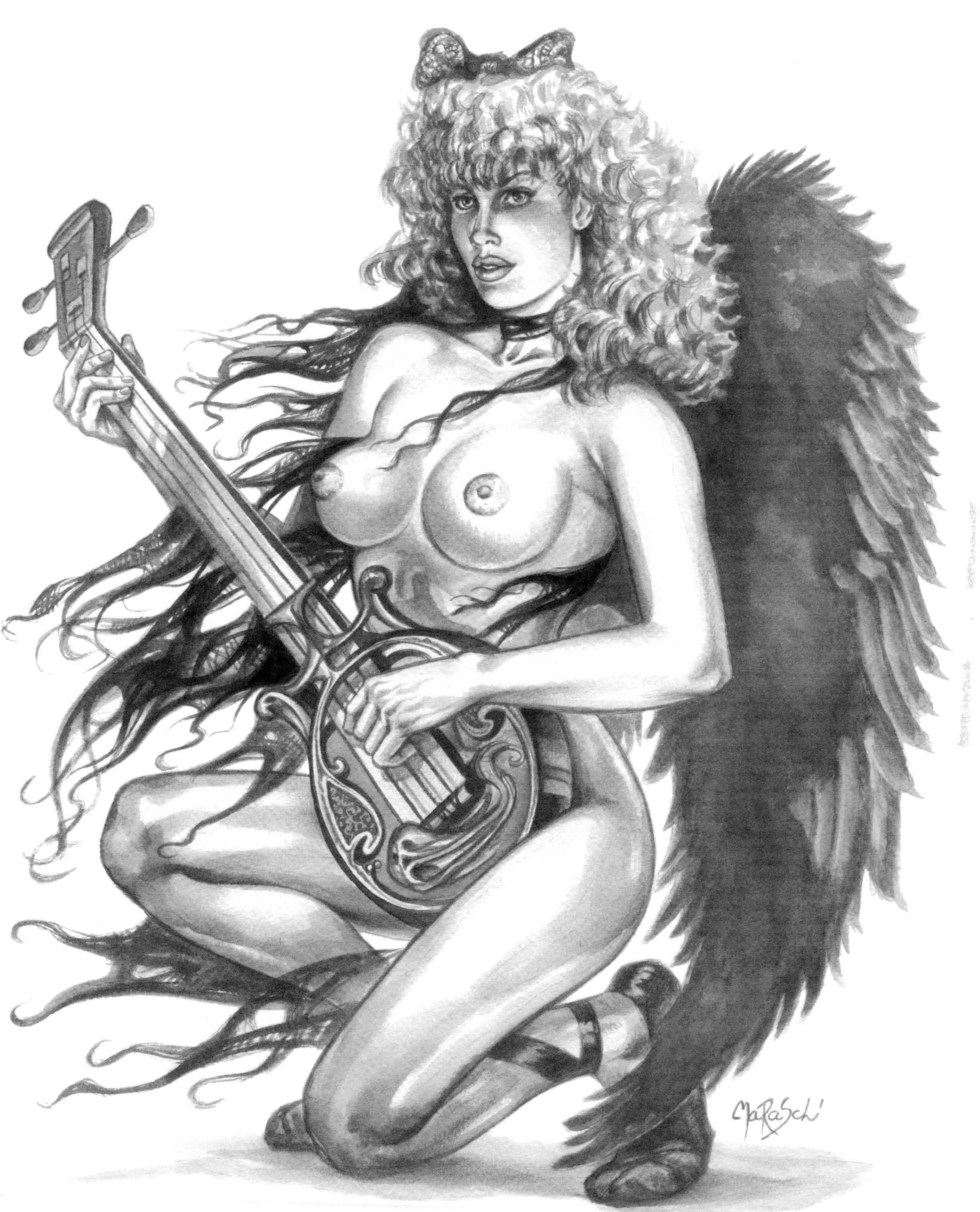

Anibal Maraschi

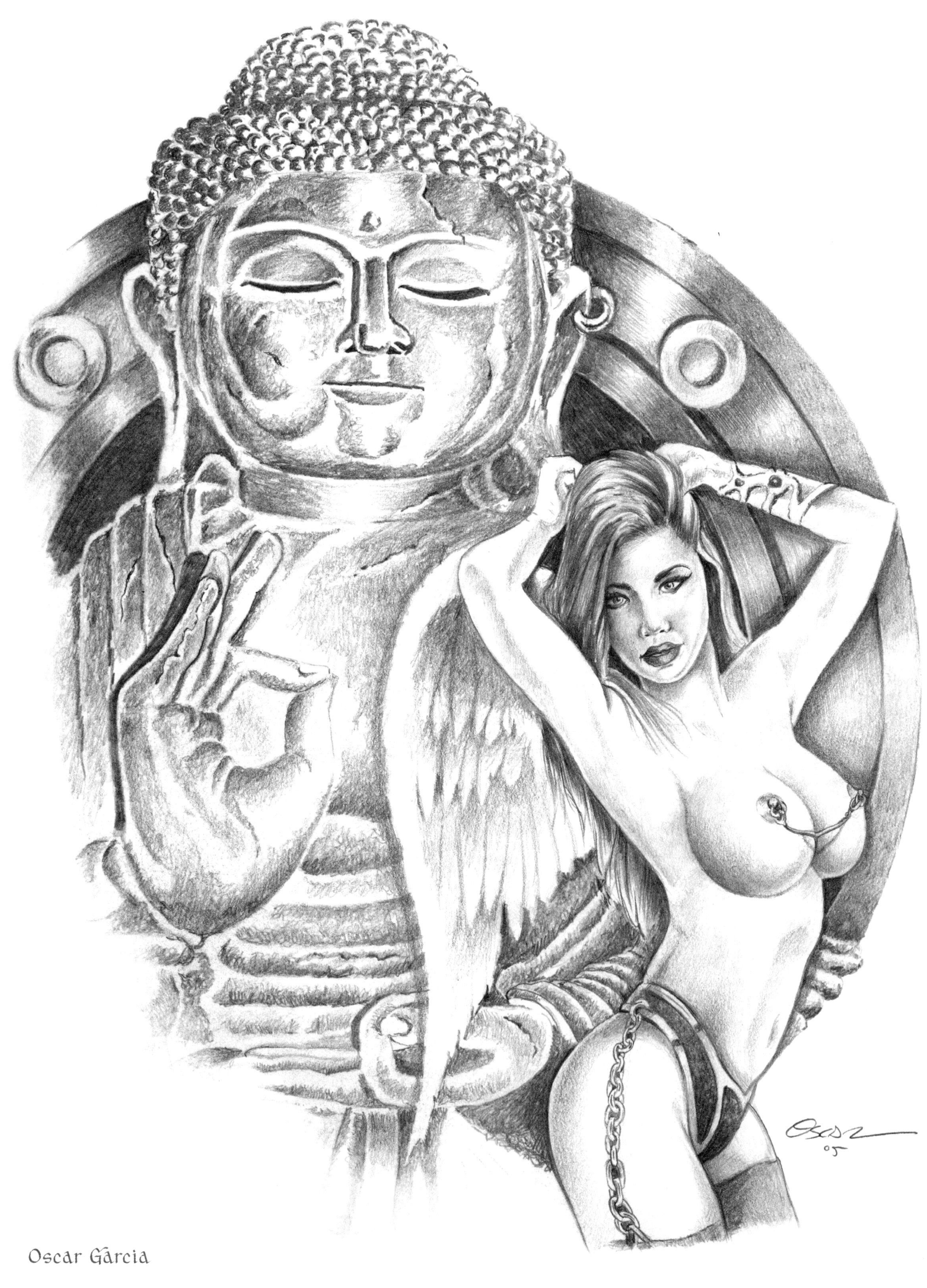

Oscar Gàrcia

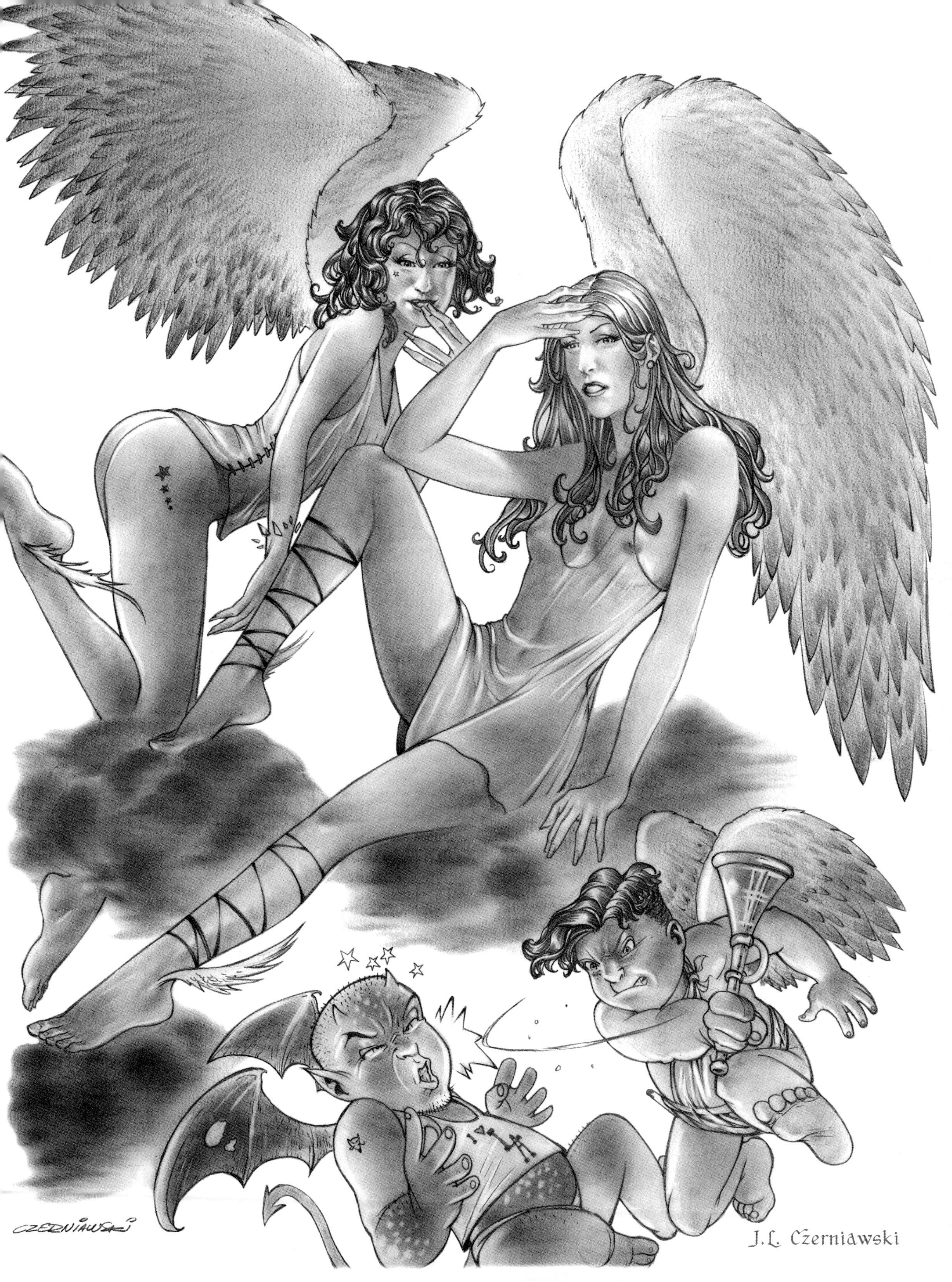
CZERNIAWSKI
J.L. Czerniawski

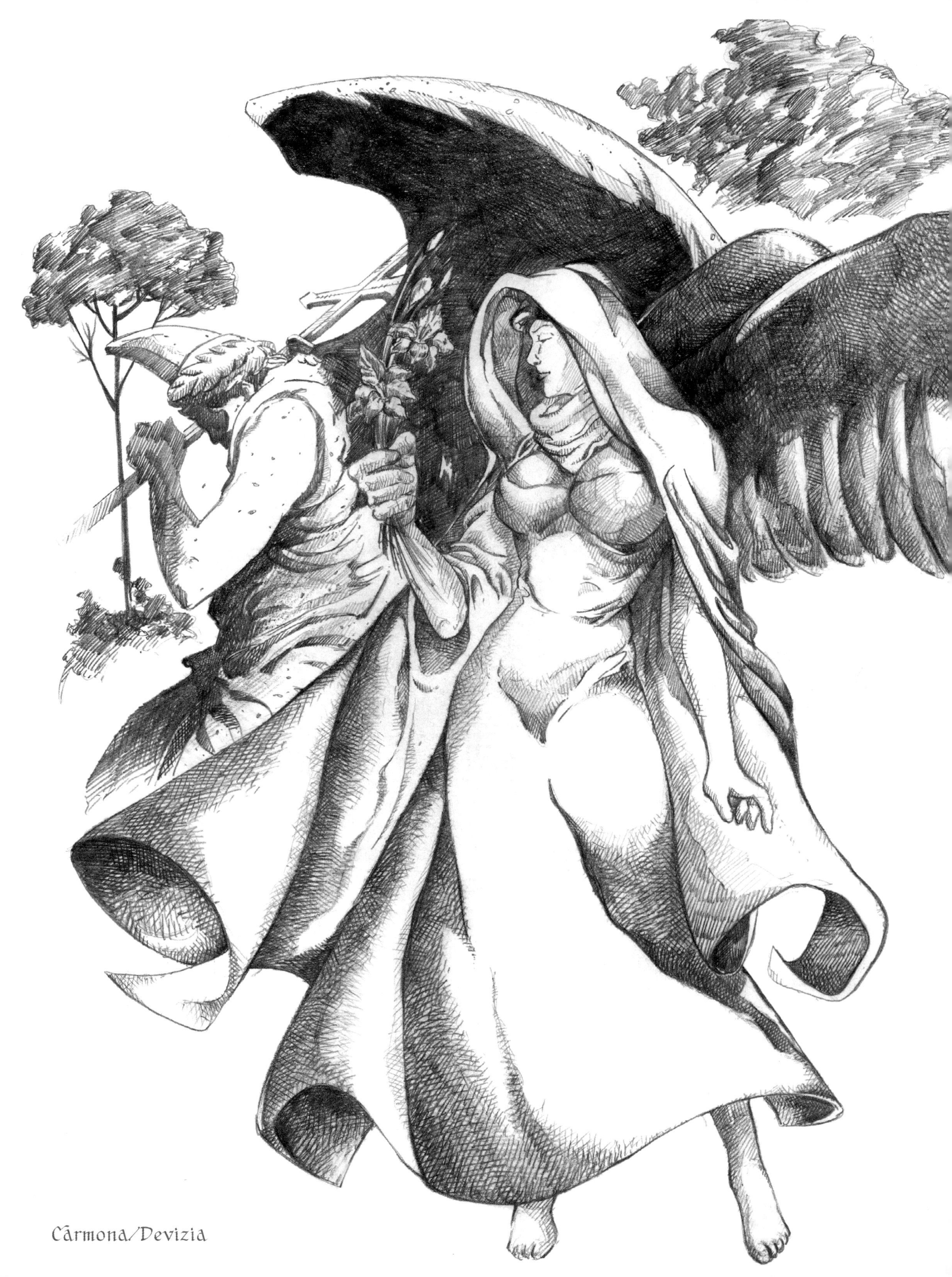
Cārmona/Devizia

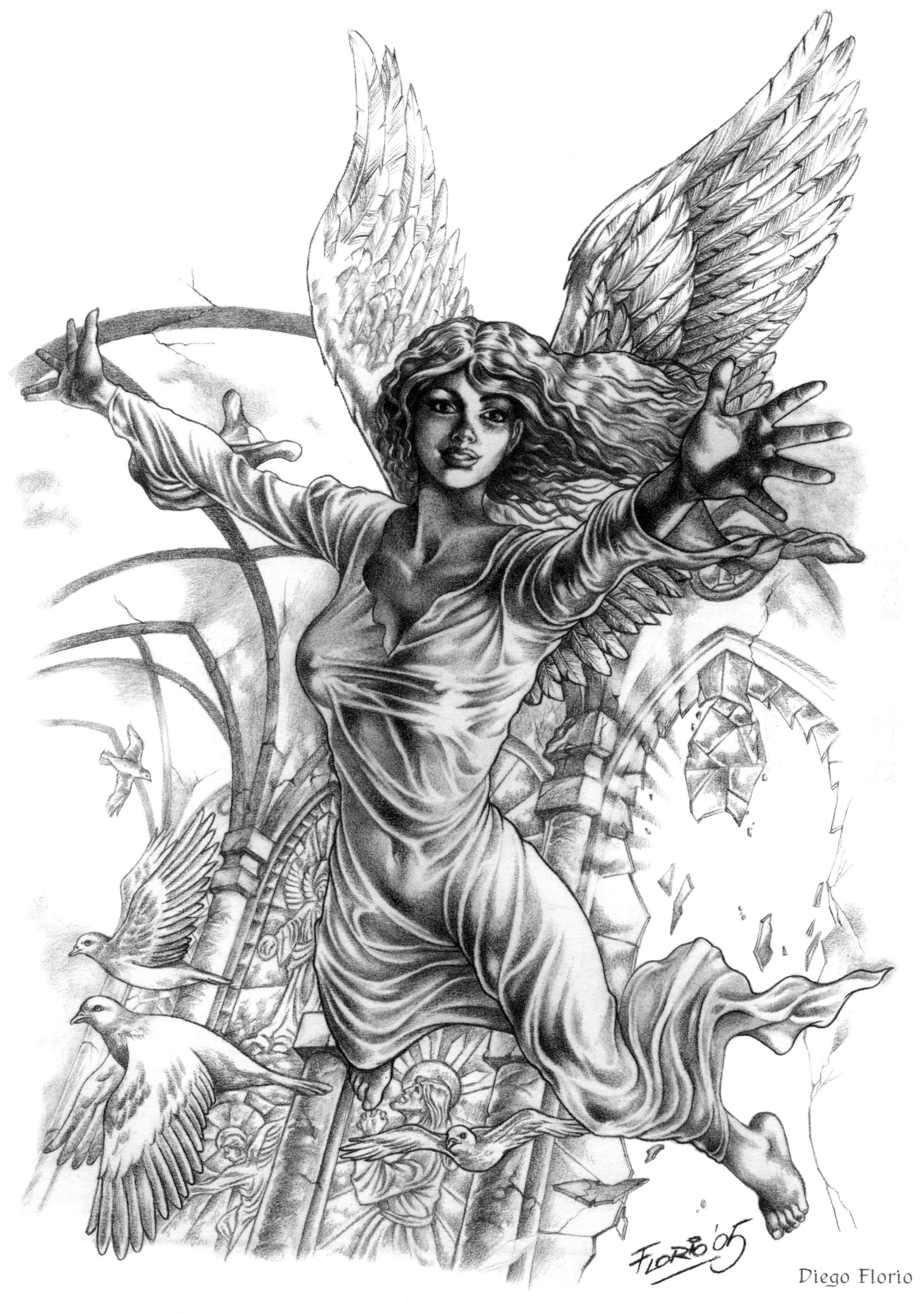

Diego Florio

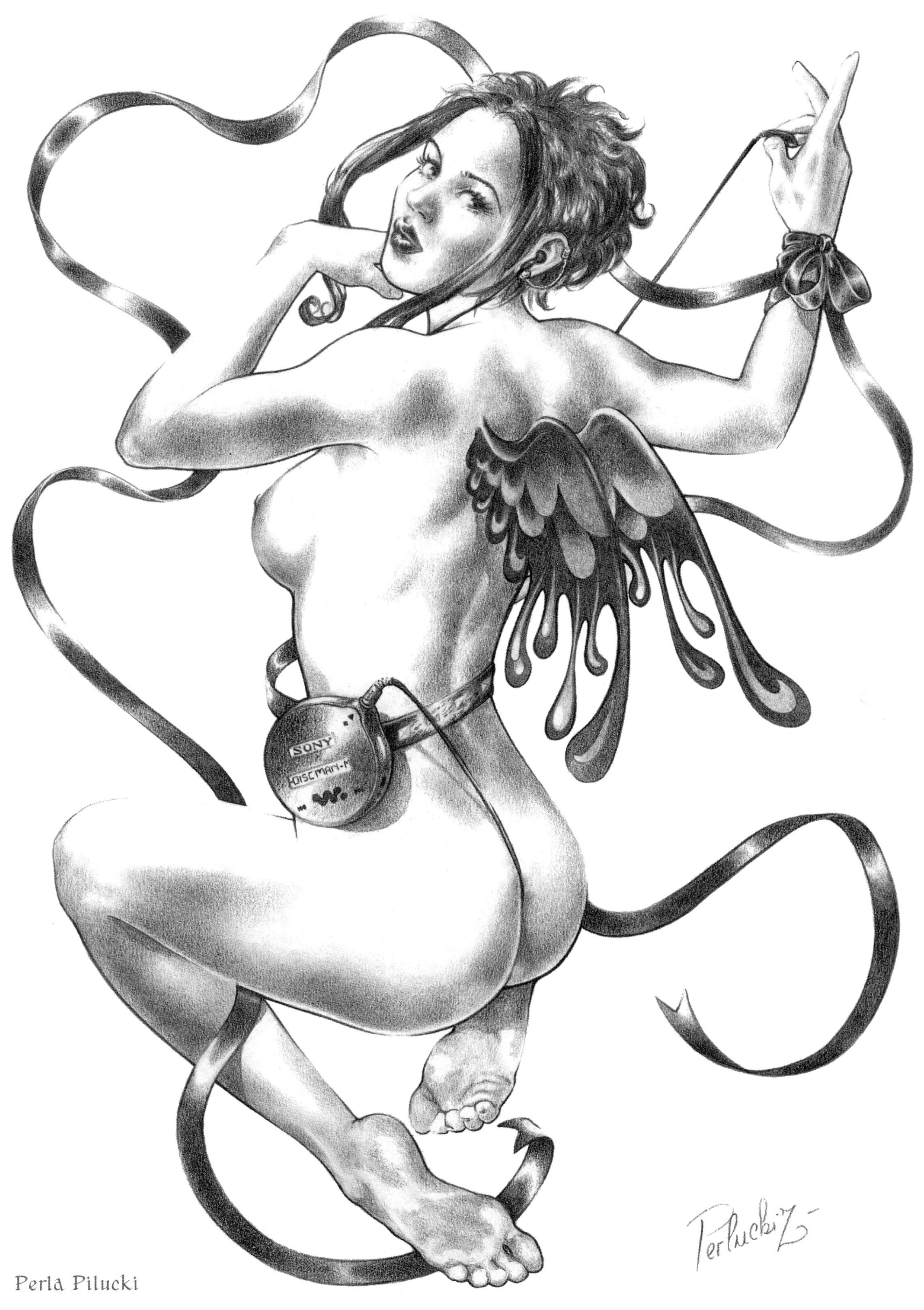

Perla Pilucki

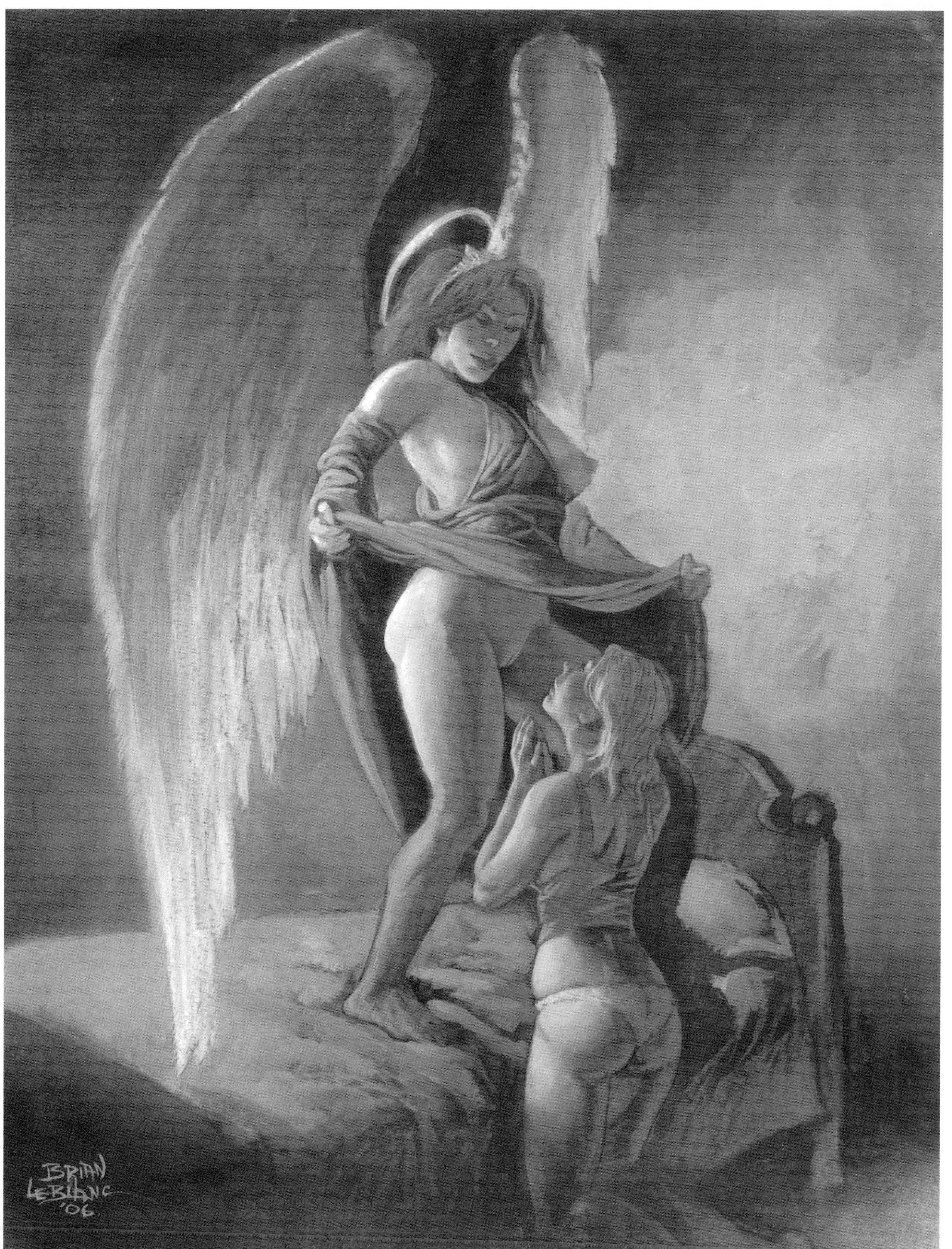

Brian LeBlanc

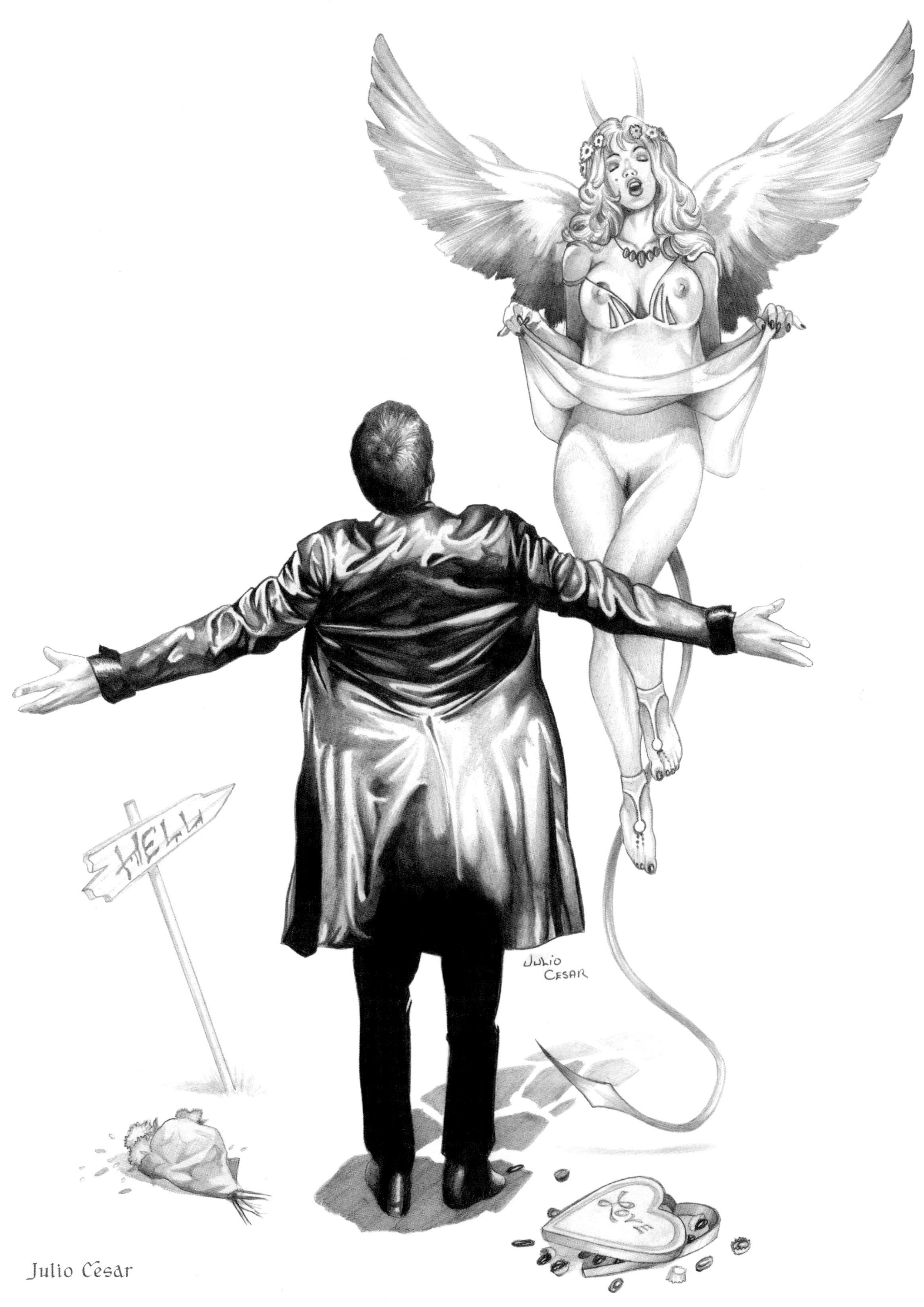

Julio César

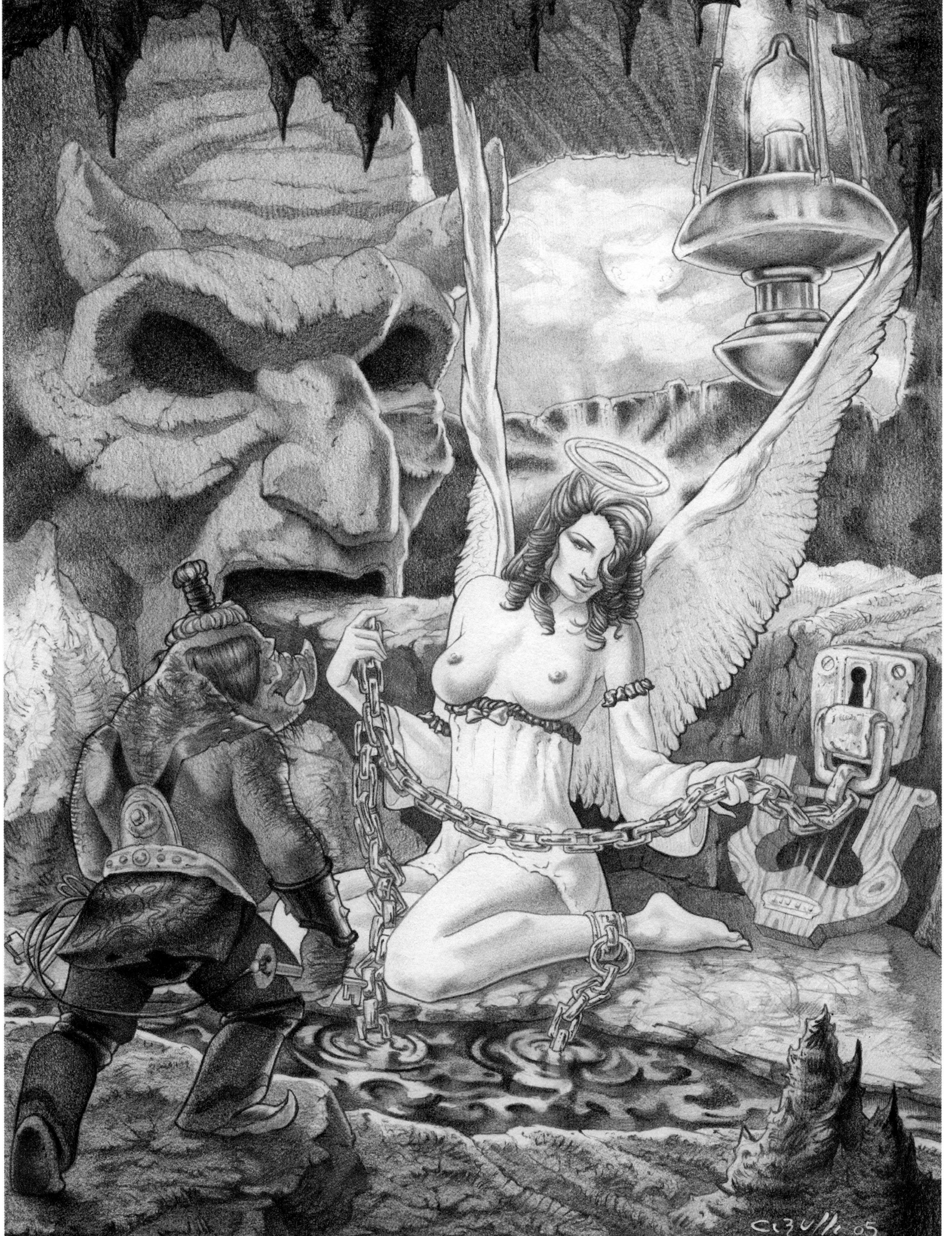

Diego Cirulli

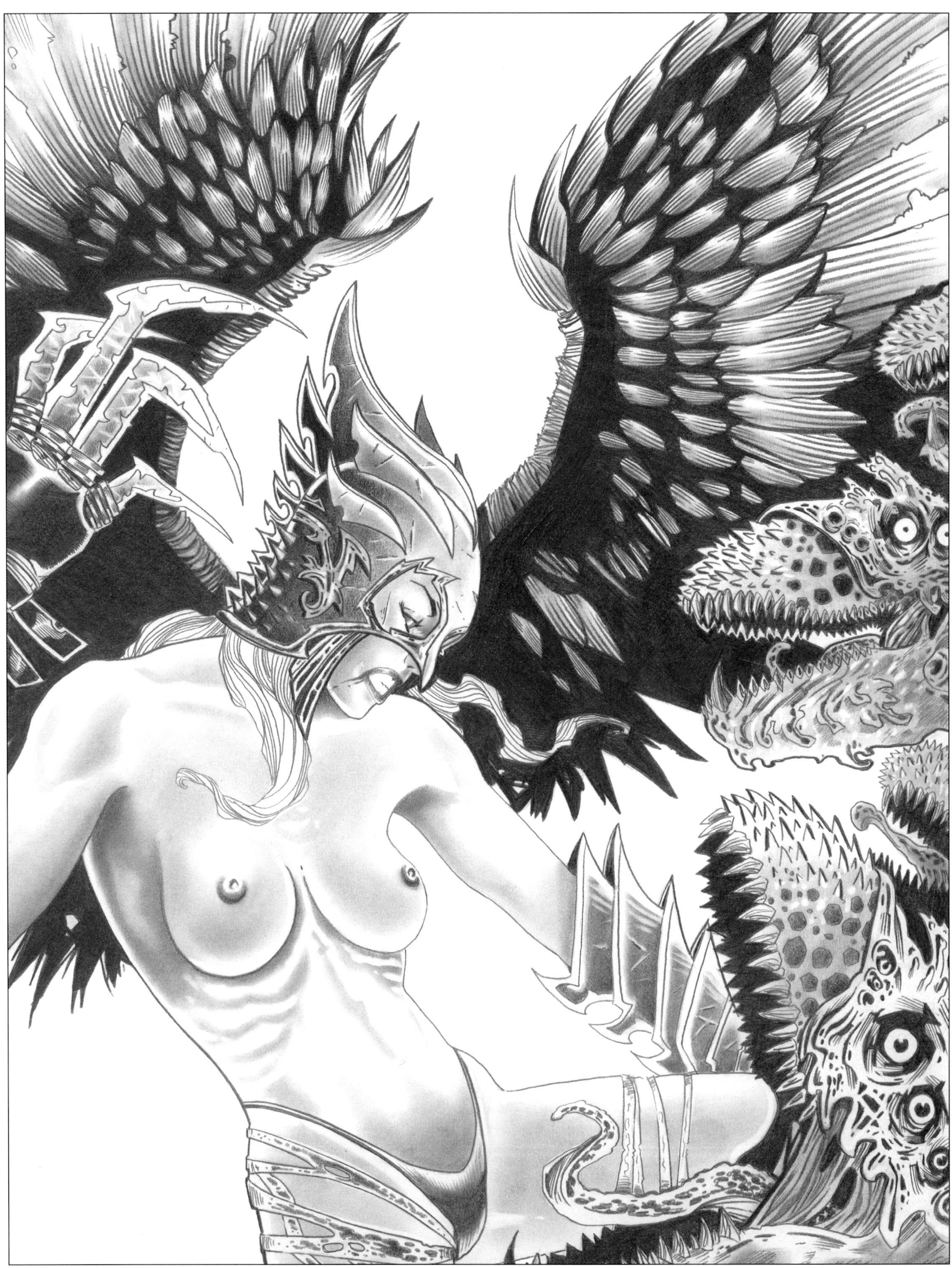

Luis Buci

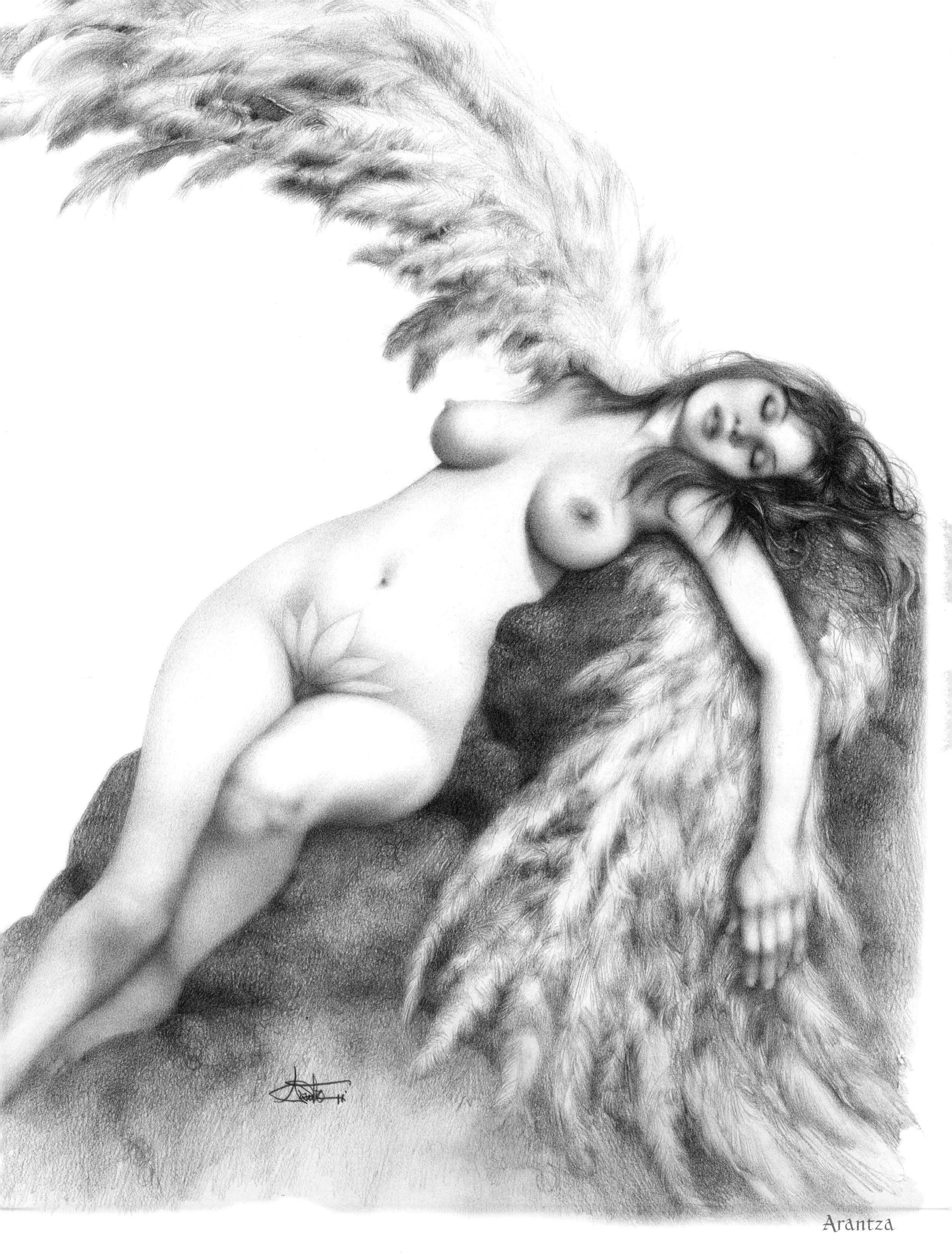

Arantza

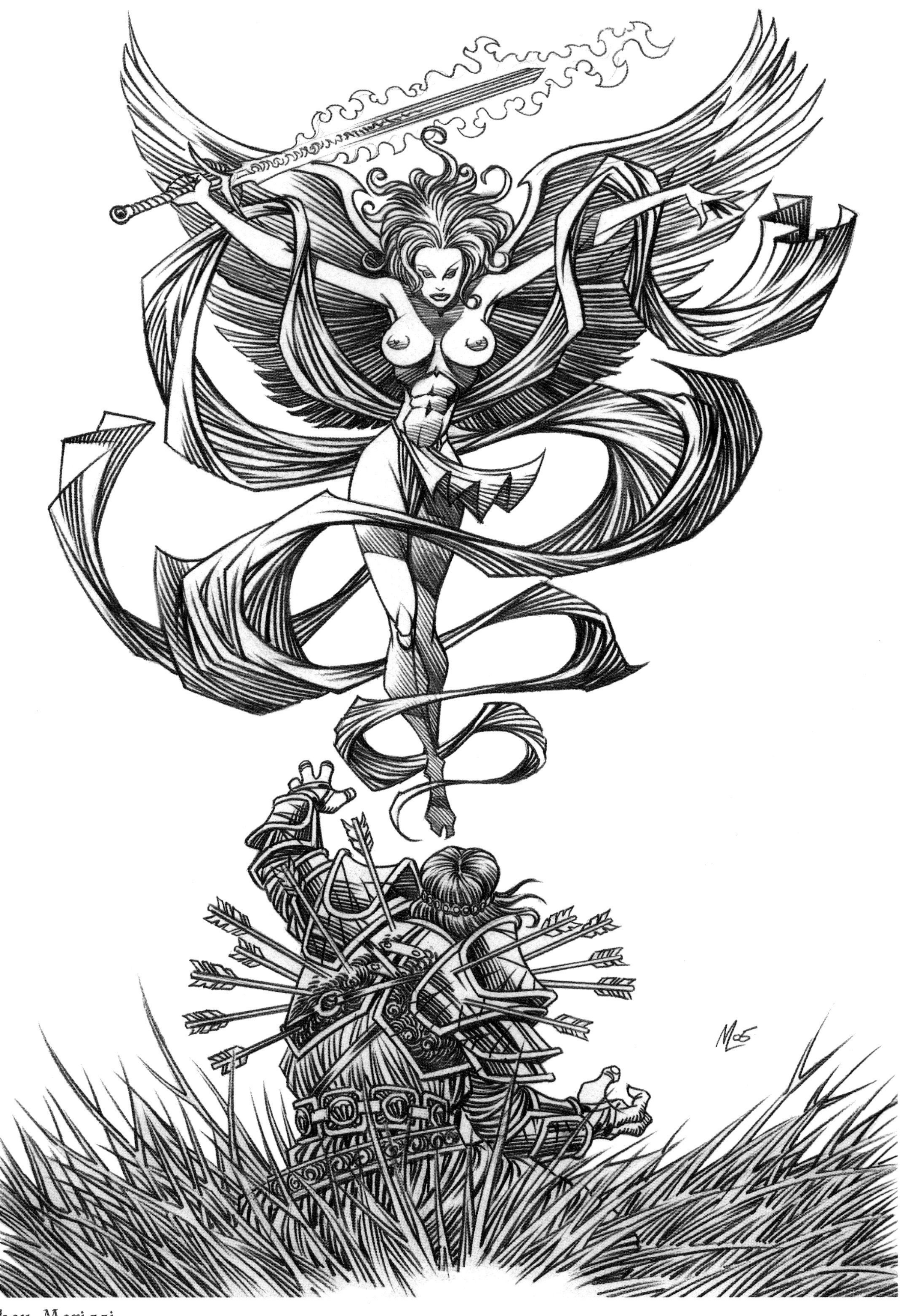

Ruben Meriggi

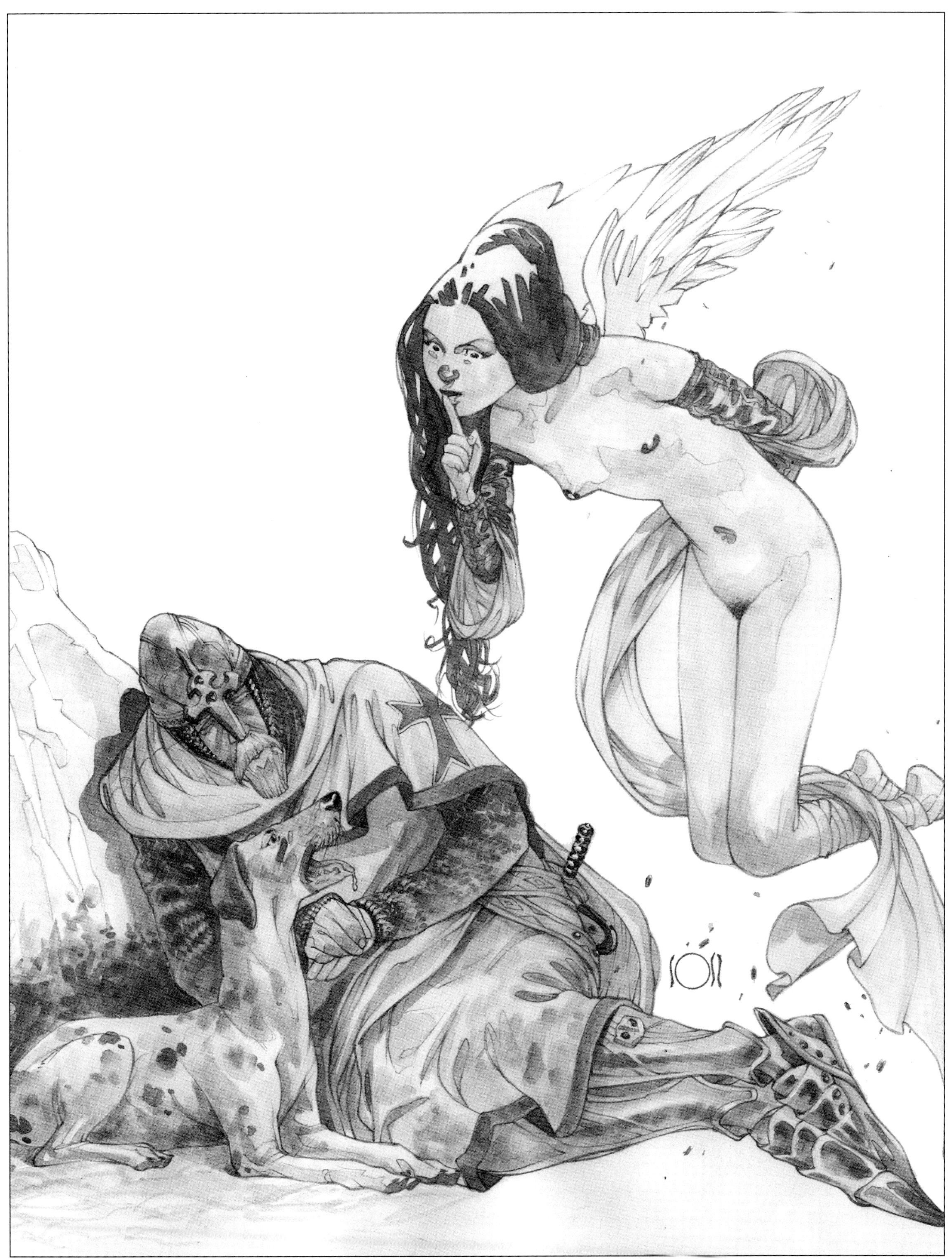

Marcelo Sosa

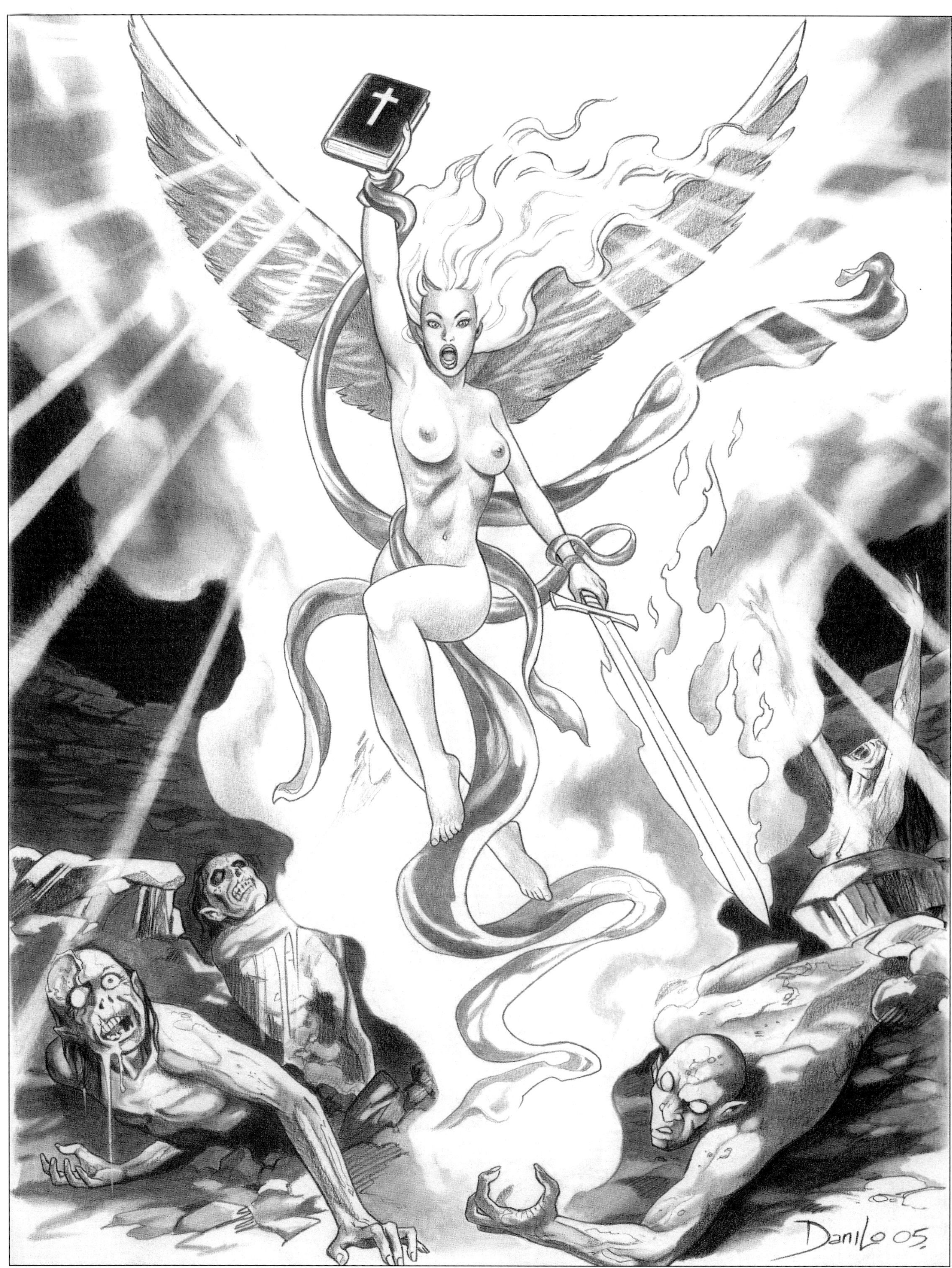

Danilo Guida

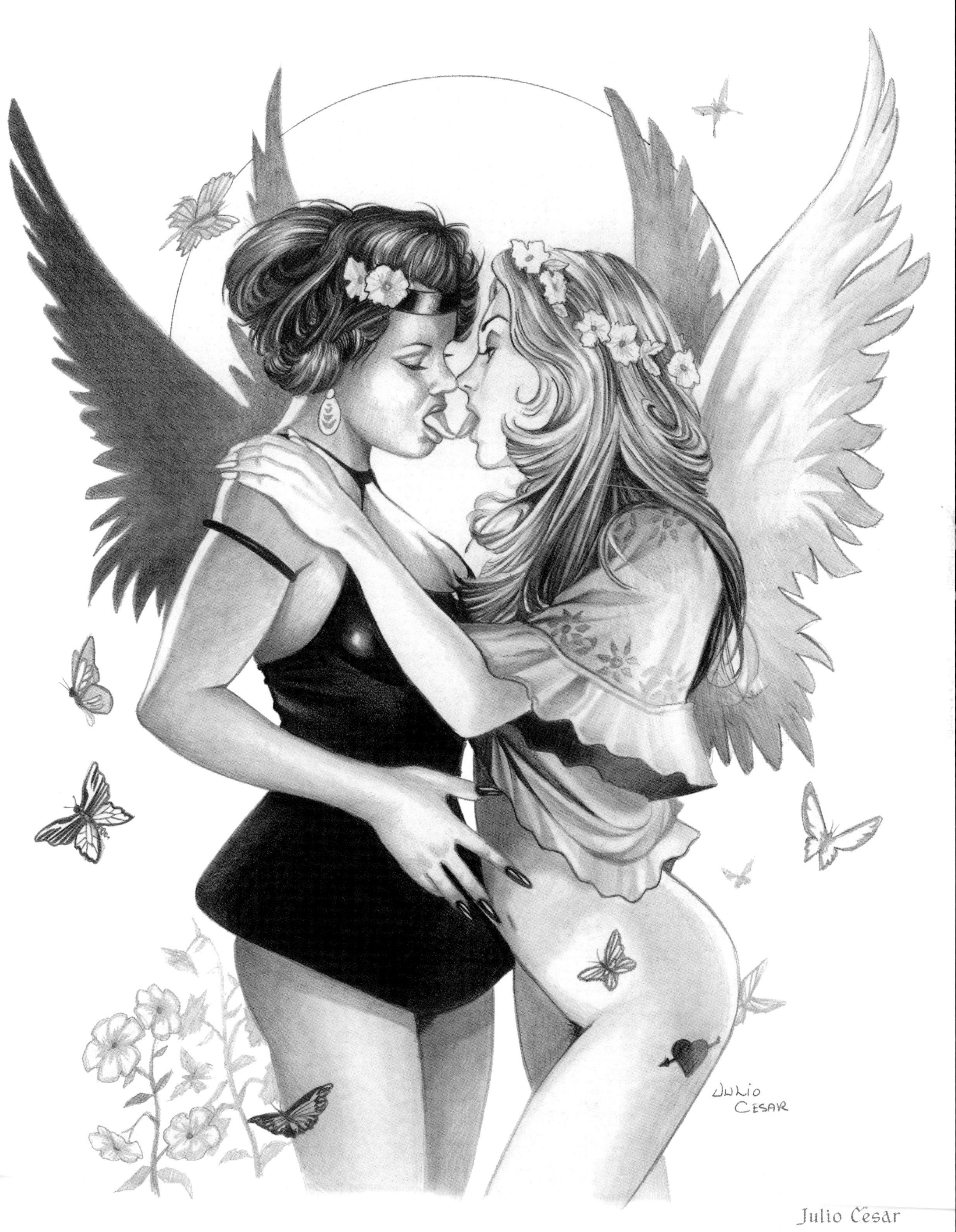

Julio César

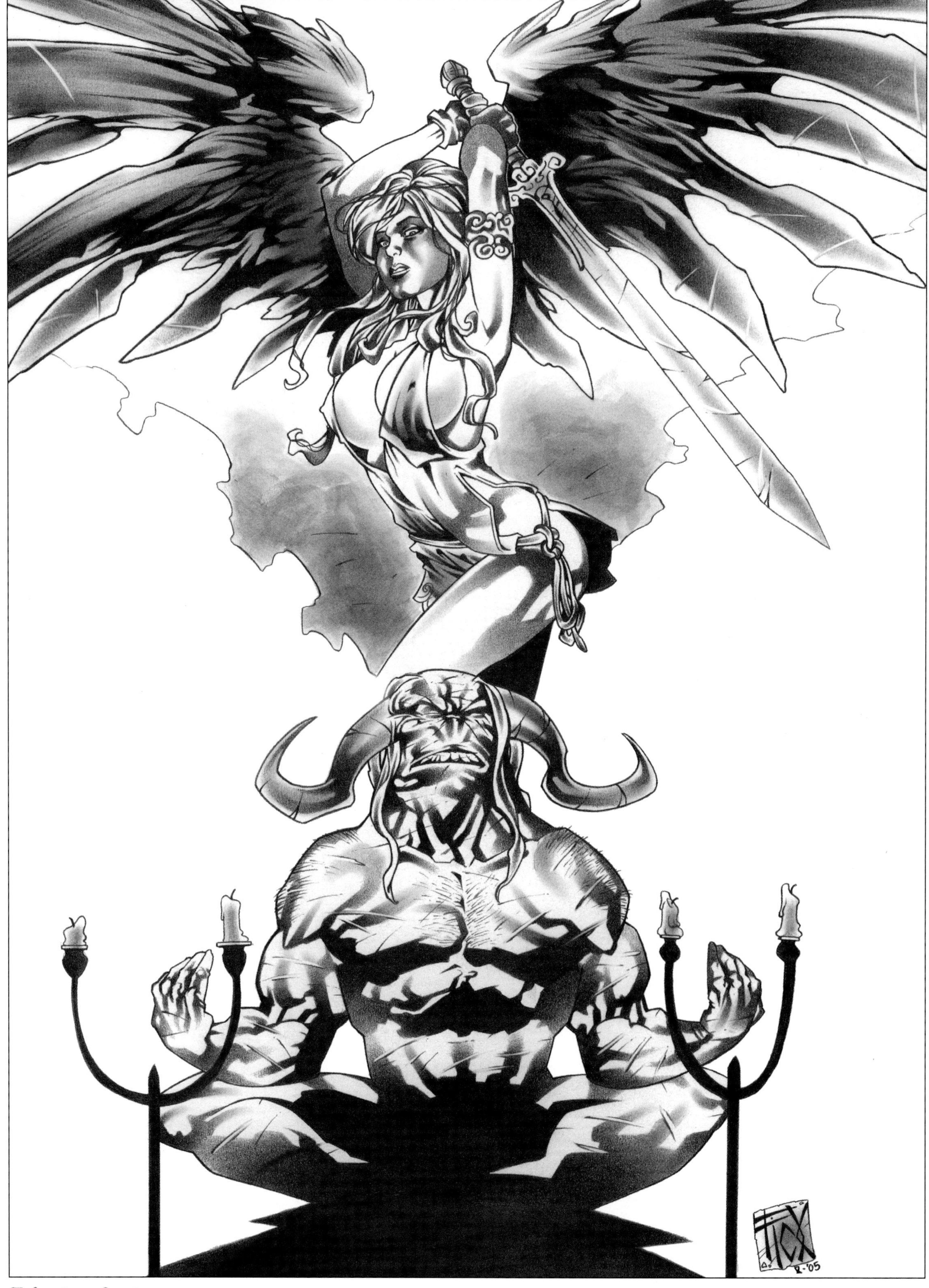

Federico Ossio

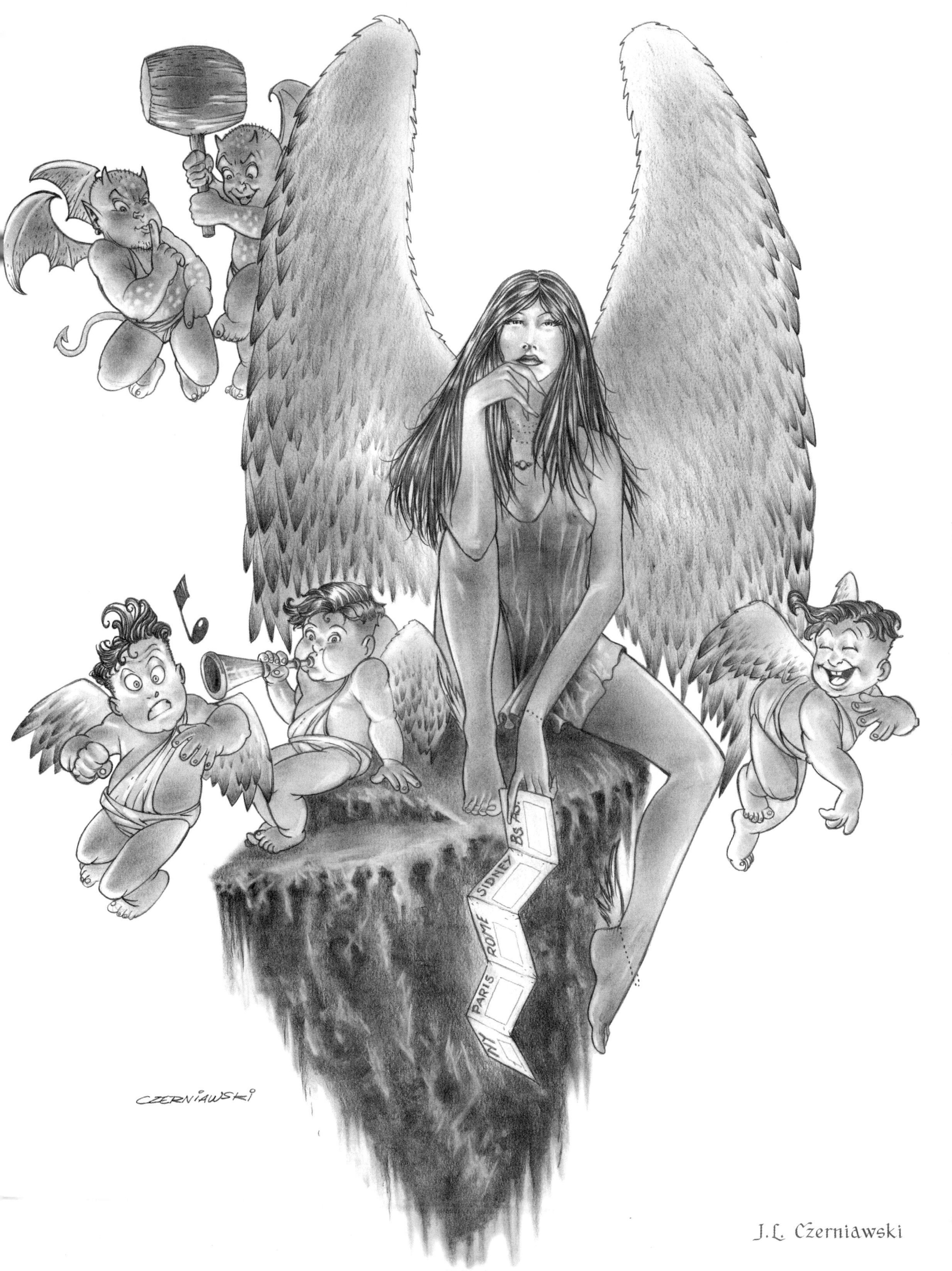
CZERNIAWSKI
BS AS.
SIDNEY
ROME
PARIS
NY
J.L. Czerniawski

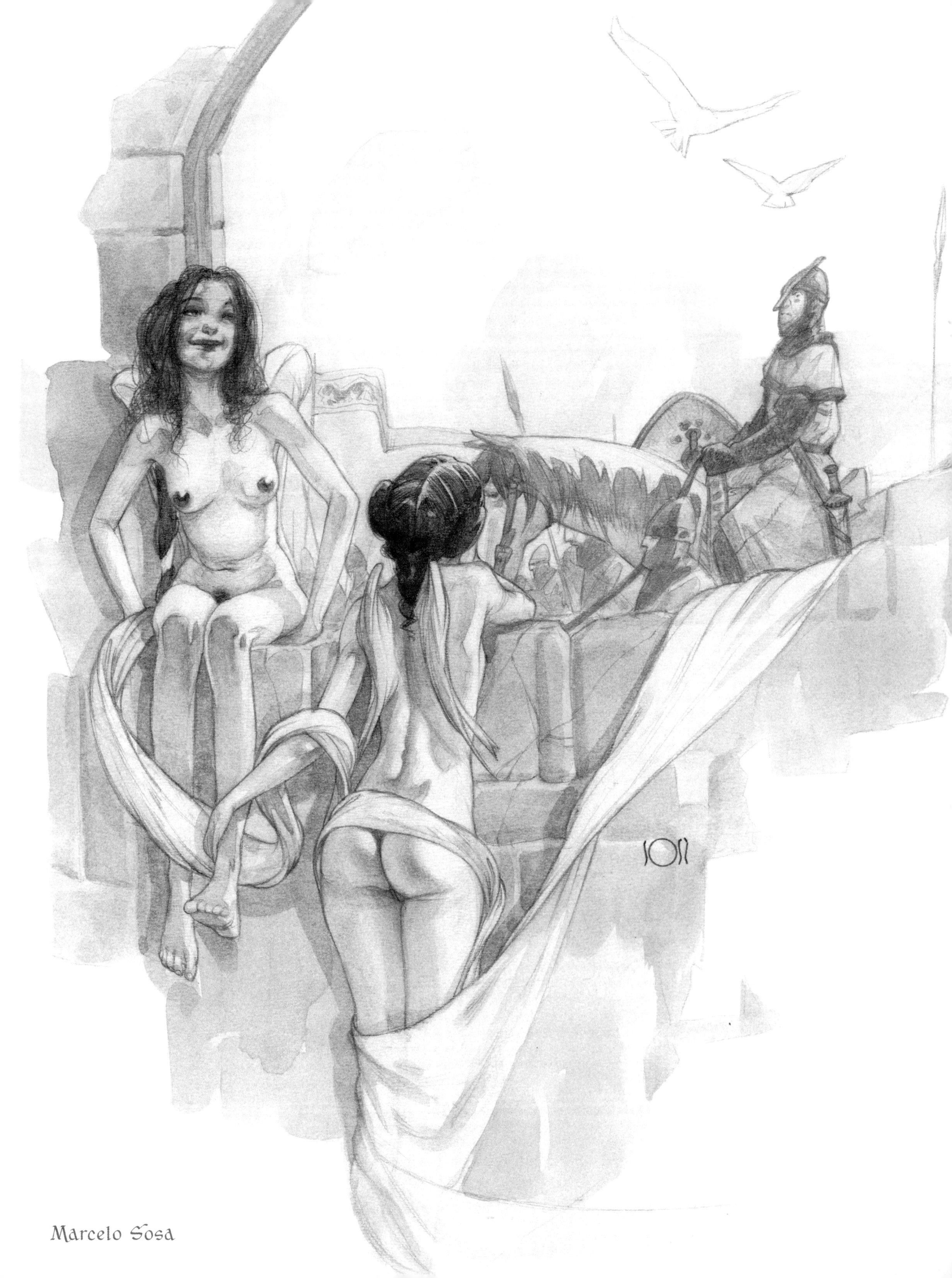

Marcelo Sosa

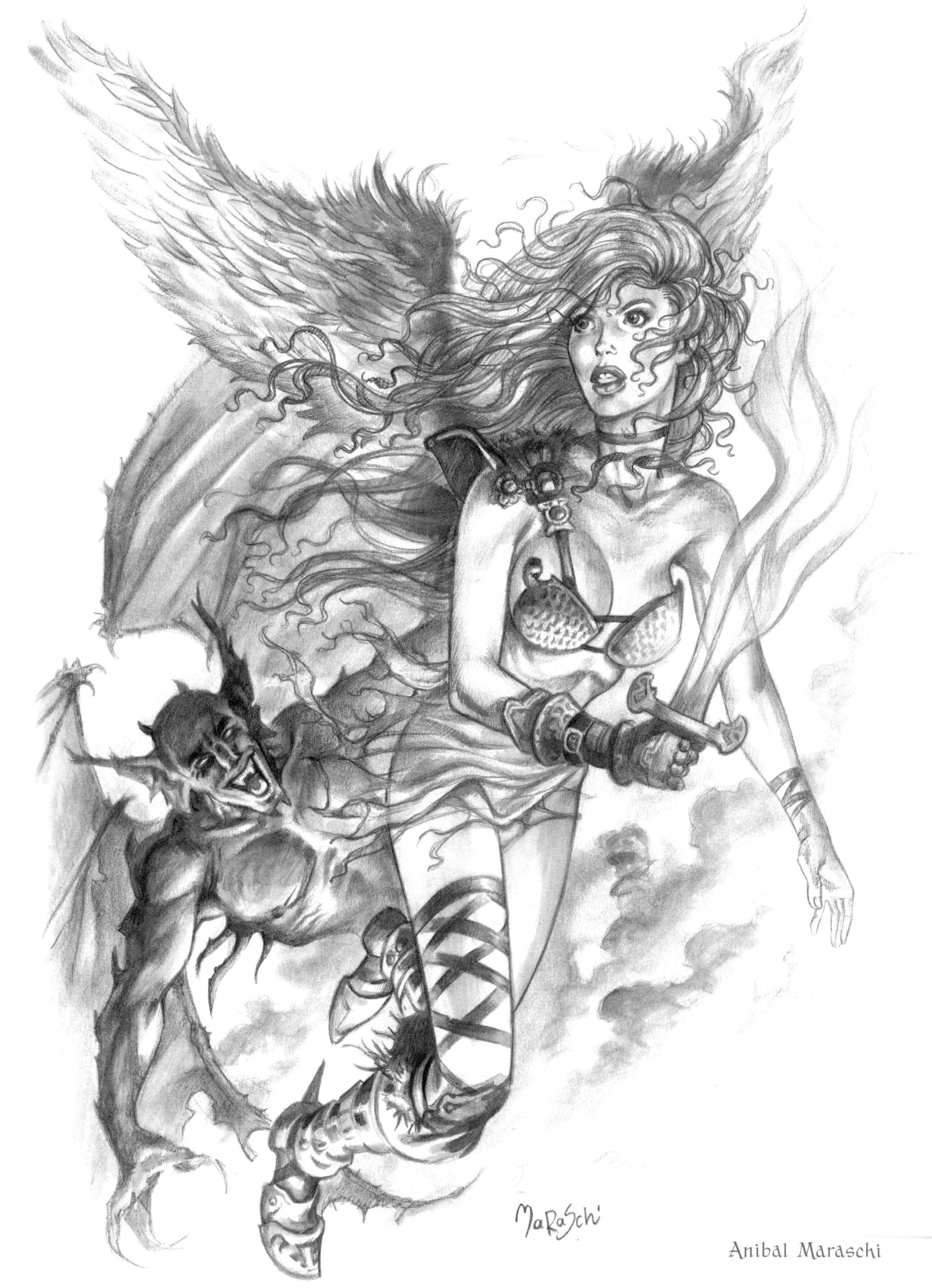
MaRaSchi
Anibal Maraschi

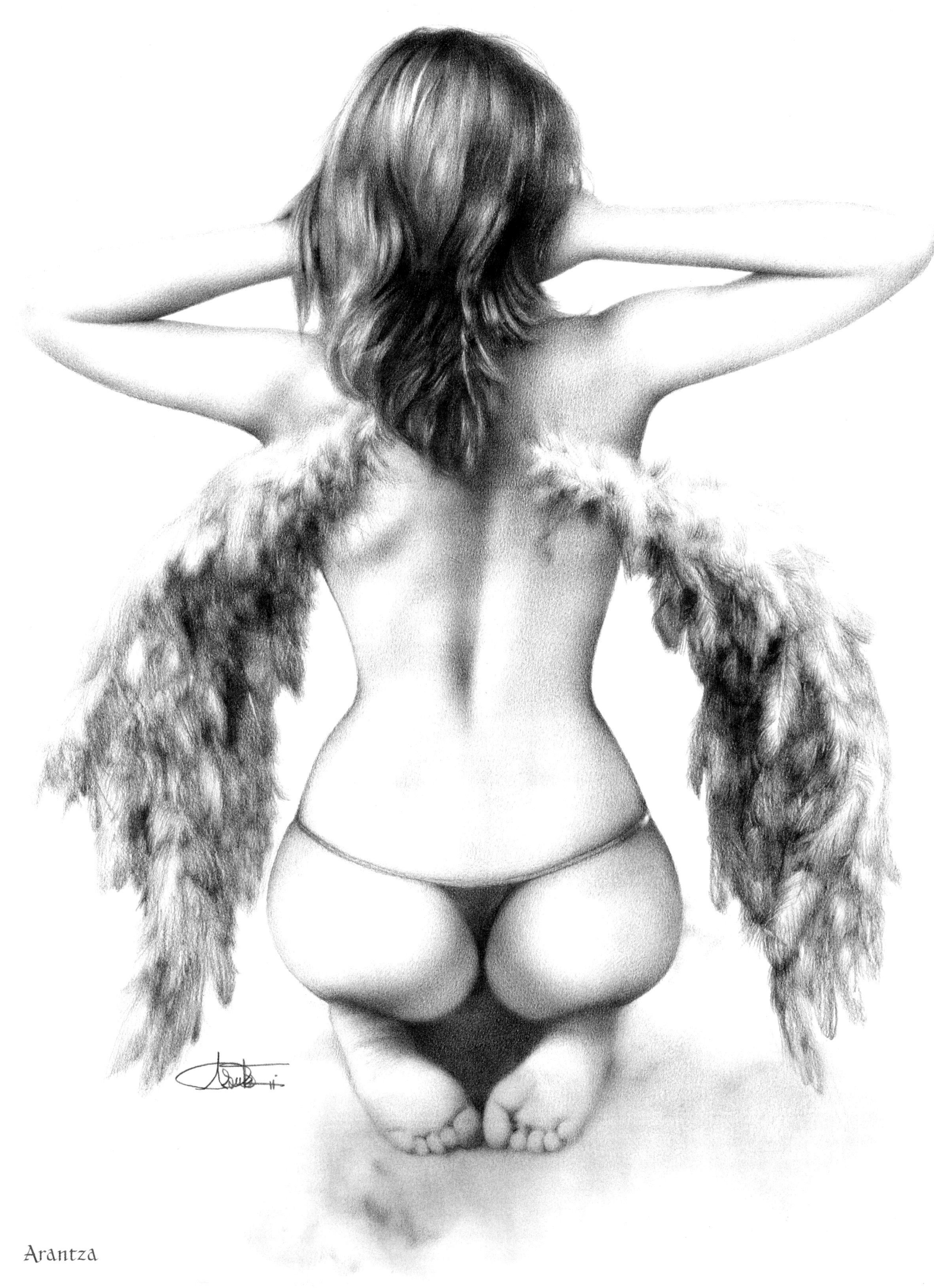

Arantza